BEYOND
CONSCIOUSNESS

BEYOND CONSCIOUSNESS

JC GORDON

Illustrations and cover drawn by Cory Van Lepreren
www.corycatures.com

Higher Consciousness image as seen by Audrey Keenan
www.angelartforhealinghearts.com

Cover image Shutterstock.com

In loving memory of my adopted parents Merle and Willard; and my father Bob McNair.

To my wonderful wife Ella, thank you for your friendship, support, love and continued encouragement.

You are the GREATEST!

To my dear friends Dorothy Ramsey, Ed and Hope Rychkun, Mike Desrochers, Paulo Frazao and Paul Jackson; thank you for your strength and support.

My hope is that you, the reader, authorize your Higher Consciousness infinite potentials to be deified in your life.

AUTHOR'S NOTE

Beyond Consciousness is the wisdom of "why life is" that was made known to me by the Higher Consciousness of life during my June 25, 1996 near death experience (NDE).

After returning from my NDE I completed a 20 year post NDE Higher Consciousness internship to understand how to best incorporate my NDE downloads for the maximum benefit of mankind.

This book is the culmination of my NDE downloads and my 20 year post NDE Higher Consciousness internship that accurately reflects their significance.

CONTENTS

PART V- APPLYING THE SECRET

PART VI- THE ENERGY PREGNANCY SECRET CONCERT

PART VII- THE SECRET VARIABLE

PART I:
THE SECRET OF LIFE

Chapter 1

My Near Death Experience

"The ultimate value of life depends upon awareness and the power of contemplation rather than upon mere survival."
Aristotle (384BC – 322BC)

STEVE JOBS, WALT DISNEY, Albert Einstein and Galileo all cracked open their imagination portal to unlock a portion of its infinite potential. In doing so, they have blessed us with their legacies.

Their legacies all began with an initial "ah-ha" awakening that morphed into their life's driving force. It was the event that put them on their imagination's pathway of inspiration and awe.

For me this began on June 25, 1996 at 1:11 p.m. I was living in Hagensborg, British Columbia, Canada. I was cutting wood with a chainsaw when it suddenly kicked back and nearly decapitated me. It sliced the left side of my throat wide open from my jawbone to my collarbone. I remember looking down and seeing my white sweatshirt turn blood red.

With the chainsaw still running and stuck to my sweatshirt, I intuitively heard a wee, small voice from within telling me, *"Everything will be okay, I have a purpose for your life."* This was the inspiration I needed to get me through what was to come.

It was astounding how that inspiration calmed me down. I didn't panic. I hollered at Young Kim, who was working with me, and motioned him to come over and help.

When he saw what happened he sprinted over to me and in his broken Korean-English asked, "What to do? What to do?"

I answered, "Turn the chainsaw off."

It was a very old chainsaw that 19 times out of 20 didn't work when the red "kill switch" was pushed; fortunately, this time it did. Young Kim turned the chainsaw off and pulled it off me.

I told Young Kim to get Steve Johnson who was driving an excavator about 50 yards away. Young Kim ran and told Steve what happened. I remember Steve turning around to see what Young Kim was talking about. When he realized what had happened, Steve immediately jumped down from his excavator and sprinted toward me.

Fortunately nothing rattled Steve; he calmly took my arm, led me to his truck and told Young Kim to call 9-1-1 right away.

We were about 45 minutes from the nearest hospital in Bella Coola. The Bella Coola Hospital is nothing more than a medical outpost. There is only one paved road in the Bella Coola Valley and after about 20 minutes Steve and I saw the ambulance speeding toward us with its lights flashing. Steve rolled down the window and waved the ambulance down. The ambulance slowed down, made a U-turn and pulled in behind us by the side of the road.

Steve told me to wait while he went to speak with the ambulance attendants. After about 30 seconds, I decided to get up and meet them at the back of the ambulance. When one of the ambulance attendants saw me, her eyes opened wide like she was seeing a dead man walking. She immediately helped me into the back of the ambulance.

The ride to the Bella Coola Hospital was another 25 minutes. Fearing I was about to pass out and die on her, the ambulance attendant asked me my name eight times. Finally when she asked me the last time, I replied, "Don't worry everything will be fine." Now she thought for sure I was delirious and about to die.

The hospital staff had been notified and they were prepared for my arrival. I remember being moved into the emergency room on the ambulance's stretcher.

At that time (1996) the Bella Coola Hospital had three doctors who rotated shifts. One of the doctors was away on vacation and had been replaced by a retired locum from Salt Spring Island. I was fortunate, for I believe he was the only one who had the confidence and ability to stitch me up. While lying on my back, the doctor was on my left and his nurse was on my right.

I recall the nurse showing the doctor an antiseptic in a sealed packet. She asked him if she should use it, but the doctor didn't know what she was holding. He leaned over me to get a closer look and asked, "What the hell is that?"

When she told him what she was holding he said, "Yeah, yeah, put it on."

The nurse opened the packet and rubbed its contents on my wound to make sure the germs and microorganisms were killed so the infection wouldn't spread.

Next, I remember the doctor attempting to thread the eye of his needle with suture thread; finally, in frustration he handed it over to the nurse. His needle looked like a fishing hook.

When he passed his needle I said, "It's all good everything will be fine." The nurse threaded the needle easily and handed it back to him.

The next thing I knew I was no longer in my body: I was separated from it. I was suddenly floating from the ceiling of the emergency room looking down at myself lying on the stretcher. The doctor was now on my right and the nurse was on my left. I remember seeing the tops of their heads. I saw my throat sliced wide open; it looked like raw meat with blood everywhere. Suddenly the doctor started moving his needle toward my wound. Just as it touched me I left the emergency room …

I was now in what can best be described as a pitch-black elevator of total silence, total darkness and total peace. I was weightless and I sensed I was moving through the cosmos of time in an upward direction. I looked up and saw a small twinkling light. At first, the light was like a star in the sky. Then it began to get larger until it became an all-encompassing white light that I passed through.

As I moved through it I had an overwhelming sense of security. I knew I was home. I sensed wherever this was; it was where I was supposed to be and where I wanted to be. There was an absolute peace about passing through the white light and I certainly didn't want to leave wherever it was I was.

I landed on a meadow at the top of a very high mountain. The grass was growing wild, the sunlight was warm and there were no clouds in the brilliant blue sky. I could see forever in every direction. Suddenly a force began guiding me; it gently touched me in what I perceived was my left elbow. However, I had no body.

I floated down the mountain—following a pathway without any cares or concerns. I didn't know where I was going but I knew that I was in a very special place. In the distance I saw a magnificent, circular, sparkling, temple-like structure. It was centered in a very large walled, gated property. I approached the wall and its large wooden gate automatically opened for me. As I entered the property, I floated past the open gate and was guided toward the temple.

As I neared the temple its front doors swung open, backwards from the left and from the right. I entered the temple. Inside there wasn't any sign of life, but energetically it felt peaceful and comforting. I was led to the stairway on the right. The walls were made of what looked like cut stone. The stones were all different sizes. As I moved up the stairway there was no handrail on my left; however, on my right there was the stone wall.

When I reached the top of the stairway, I turned left and made my way down the hallway as there was no place to go on the right. First, I went past a room on the left. The door was open. The room was barren except for four "human like" entities sitting on the floor and facing each other in a small, tight circle. I sensed they were praying or meditating. I couldn't make out any discernible features on them. I continued down the hallway and saw a room on the right with an open door. There was no life in this room, it was a vast library of what I thought were books. I went down the hallway a little further and entered the next door on the right. As I entered the room I went through a veil and knew I has been here before.

I continued down the hallway and saw a room on the right with an open door. There was no life in this room, it was a vast library of what I thought were books.

I went down the hallway a little further and entered the next door on the right. As I entered the room I went through a veil and knew I has been here before.

I began to experience a warmth and presence that morphed into a cloud of countless individual particles. It was like the snow on a television screen. It also released the soothing fragrance of nature, like a field after a shower. For a split second I saw the face of my maternal grandfather in the cloud, which provided me with an extra sense of peace and tranquility. I was at total peace and felt a reverence I could not remember having before.

CHAPTER 2

BACK TO SCHOOL

"For there is nothing hidden that will not be disclosed,
and nothing concealed that will not be known or brought
out into the open." Luke 8:17
Jesus Christ (4BC – 30AD)

SUDDENLY I STARTED TO RECEIVE "collective zings."
Collective zings were from all six violet stars at once.
They would release individual violet colored lightning
bolts that formed one huge bolt that zinged me right
between the eyes.
My first collective zing revealed, "I am the Higher
Consciousness of everything. It is time to reveal myself.
This is why you are here. Come."

I was led into the cloud of countless individual
particles. Inside it morphed into a lab. It was not
a sophisticated lab; in fact, it reminded me of my
high school chemistry lab. It was rectangular and I
went into it with Higher Consciousness. I became an
onlooker from about half way up the back wall.

There was a blackboard on the front wall with a teacher's counter also at the front. A black counter wrapped around the two outside walls and the back wall below me. There was an unopened window on the back wall to my right. There were no doors. In the middle of the room were two empty student desks, one to my right and one to my left.

Suddenly the violet hexagram of Higher Consciousness appeared in the middle of the room, about six feet above the front counter and it hovered here and began to communicate with me again.

It said, "Welcome to the essence of who I am." I was again being downloaded directly from the Source's mouth. "Everything began right here. I will change into a form you are familiar with so you can understand."

Suddenly, Higher Consciousness began releasing small violet lightning sparks and violet lightning bolts in every direction out of its hexagram self. They were not zinging me; they were small flashes. For my benefit, it transformed itself into a more familiar form...

First, its head appeared in a violet colored brilliance that shimmered and continuously flashed and changed its violet spectrum colors from light to dark. It was as though I was watching a live MRI of the brain before me. Its hexagram shape began to lose its corners and became more circular.

Once its head was complete, it began to organize itself. It started by dividing into two halves. Its division started at its outer twelve o'clock point at the top of its head. It made a slight "S-like" curve that ran right through the middle of its head to about six o'clock at its head's base. The right side became a dark violet hue and the left side was light violet in color. Both sides continued to release violet sparks and violet lightning bolts; both sides were very much alive and transforming themselves.

Then, without warning, in each half two smaller circles appeared. The first, in the darker right side, was about two-thirds of the way down and the second in the lighter left side was about two-thirds of the way up. They developed eyelashes and eyelids, which opened to reveal eyes. Its eyes continuously changed color from dark red to light violet (including orange, yellow, green and blue).

Unexpectedly, came an angelic body that had two arms, two hands thumbs and three fingers on each hand. Its body had a violet radiance that shimmered its complete violet color spectrum. As it continued to float above the front counter, its body gently undulated from side to side like a fish out of water while its head remained stationary.

Then, its right eye sent out a dark violet lightning bolt zing that crackled and moved very slowly toward the vacant desk on my right. When it touched the desk, a male image appeared in the seat. Its form was also angelic in appearance. It had a head, two arms, hands and fingers and a body shaped like Higher Consciousness but smaller. It did not have any other distinguishable features and it shimmered in a deep violet brilliance. Its features gave the appearance of a young man approximately 16 years old. It had mid-length blondish, brown, wavy hair and was very handsome and expressionless. It also had a beaming dark violet crystalline countenance.

Then, Higher Consciousness left eye began to send out a similar crackling violet lightning bolt zing, which moved slowly toward the vacant desk on my left. When it touched the desk, a young girl appeared in the seat. She had the same similar angelic form as the male image, but was slightly smaller than the male image. She looked to be around 12 years old, and also had a head, two arms, hands and fingers. She had long dark hair and a lighter violet intensity to her form. What I remember most was her infectious smile. She also possessed a beaming light violet crystalline countenance.

Next, I watched Higher Consciousness begin to speak from above the front counter. While lifting its arms up, it declared to its male and female forms that, "I am the Force of all that is."

Then, I watched as Higher Consciousness floated toward the male form and placed its left hand on its head and bestowed it with the name: "Lucifer."

It then turned and left Lucifer and floated toward the female form just a few feet away. It hovered above the female form and placed its right hand on her head. She looked down and closed her eyes. Higher Consciousness then bestowed her with the name: "Lucy."

It then floated back to its initial position a few feet above the front counter and announced to Lucifer and Lucy, "You are my energy eyes that will complete my energy pregnancy... Lucifer you are my male consciousness energy. Lucy you are my female consciousness energy. Combined you make me whole."

CHAPTER 3

THE ENERGY MATRIX

"How wonderful that we have met with a paradox. Now we have some hope of making progress."
Niels Bohr (1885 – 1962)

HIGHER CONSCIOUSNESS next began creating its energy matrix.

Higher Consciousness' 3D energy matrix

Higher Consciousness disclosed while creating its energy matrix that this is "my energy pulse."

I watched as Lucifer and Lucy absorbed everything Higher Consciousness was doing. They were like sponges soaking it all in.

Higher Consciousness then asked if there were any questions to which Lucifer asked, "Is this your power?"

Higher Consciousness replied, "This is my protection so nothing can harm my energy pregnancy."

As it answered, Lucifer temporarily dropped his gaze while Lucy kept watching.

Higher Consciousness finished its energy matrix by unleashing violet lightning zings through the tips of its left and right index fingers. The zings completed its splendor and magnificence on the blackboard.

There were ten strategically designed circular shaped seals on the energy matrix to which Higher Consciousness pronounced, "I will unlock my seals to release the master forces of my energy pregnancy. Behind each seal is one of my energy pregnancy master forces which are all safely stored in my energy mind. When I have energetically unlocked all of my energy seals my ten master forces will have been directed into my energy womb to complete my energy pregnancy."

CHAPTER 4

UNLOCKING THE ENERGY MATRIX

HEARING NO FURTHER QUESTIONS, Higher Consciousness assumed its levitating position above the front counter. Facing us, it lifted its arms up until they were parallel with the ground. It pointed its left and right index fingers at each other and sent out violet lightning zings from them. When the violet lightning zings met, an explosion formed a mega 3D, see-through empty sphere, to which Higher Consciousness exclaimed, "This is my energy womb and it's time for you (Lucy and Lucifer) to understand how my ten master force powers will work in it."

Higher Consciousness then drifted toward its energy matrix on the front blackboard; reached out its left index finger and unleashed a violet energy zing that unlocked its first energy seal.

◯

The first seal

It told us that "My first master force is the power that conceives my energy fetus in my energy womb." We all watched as it directed its first violet colored master force out of its energy mind, and into its energy womb.

Suddenly its barren energy womb experienced a massive explosion from within. It then advised us "This is my energy conception."

We watched the explosion form a round glowing red ball that took up all the space within Higher Consciousness' energy womb. It then began to shrink into a tiny, twinkling red light that moved to a nine o'clock position in the energy womb. We than watched a limitless number of other tiny twinkling red lights appear and connect in the energy womb to form a small twinkling red light energy fetus. The fetus had a miniature head and miniature body similar to that of the Higher Consciousness.

Higher Consciousness then motioned to Lucifer and proclaimed, "You will aid me in completing my conception."

Lucifer asked, "How will I know what to do?"

To which Higher Consciousness responded, "You are my all-knowing left eye that I have made see. You will know what to do."

Lucifer sat back in his seat and I saw a look of peace and comfort come over him.

With Higher Consciousness' first master force in place, it next unlocked its second energy seal from its energy matrix. Its second energy seal burst open and released its second master force from its energy matrix.

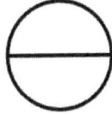

The second seal

"This is my master force that begins my energy fetus' gestation."

We saw that when Higher Consciousness directed its second master force into its energy womb, its energy fetus grew ever so slightly in size.

Suddenly in the top half of the energy womb, a violet sun appeared. Higher Consciousness used its right index finger, pointed to the violet sun, turned to Lucy and said, "This is you."

Higher Consciousness then turned to Lucifer and articulated, "You will also be supporting me with the implementation of this master force."

It paused and waited for questions.

With no question it turned and floated back to the front blackboard. I watched Lucy and Lucifer as it unlocked its third energy seal from its energy matrix.

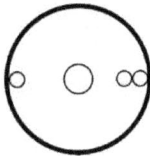

The third seal

When opened, we witnessed Higher Consciousness' energy fetus grow again in its energy womb as this master force also was directed by Higher Consciousness into its energy womb.

It next told us that "This master force continues my energy fetus' gestation."

It then explained that "This seals four circular windows will transition my angel energy threads back and forth between my energy fetus' physical realm in my energy womb and my divine realm in my energy mind."

Higher Consciousness turned to Lucifer and said, "This master force will again require your assistance in my energy fetus."

I observed Lucifer nod his approval back to Higher Consciousness.

With its third master force now unleashed and directed into its energy womb, it floated back toward the blackboard and sent violet energy zings from its left index finger to its energy matrix that unlocked its fourth energy seal.

It said, "This master force ends my energy fetus' gestation."

The fourth seal

Higher Consciousness then added, "Lucifer you must also complete this."

After a short delay, it again asked if there were any questions. Lucy confirmed that as each of Higher Consciousness' energy seals was being unlocked, she could see her role being played out before her. It revealed what she had to do; she only had to follow its lead.

When Lucy finished speaking, Lucifer took it one step further and insisted that he start now. Higher Consciousness replied, "Your time will come after I reveal the unlocking of all my energy seals."

I watched as Lucy and Lucifer anxiously awaited their unlocking.

Higher Consciousness faced us and next unleashed its violet power from its left and right index fingers to reveal its energy womb again. Its energy fetus was now full term in size

It turned to Lucifer and thanked him for his forthcoming efforts that will complete its energy fetus conception and gestation. Lucifer was told "at this moment he will rest."

Lucifer nodded while Lucy could hardly contain her excitement.

Higher Consciousness then proclaimed, "My energy labor must now begin."

With this, it unlocked its fifth energy seal from its energy matrix.

The fifth seal

Higher Consciousness said, "This master force is

my energy pregnancies breaking of water moment for Lucy."

It then unlocked its sixth energy seal. This time it did so with a zing from the index finger on its right hand.

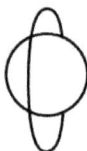

The sixth seal

Higher Consciousness stated, "This master force begins my energy fetus' energy labor and deification."

Higher Consciousness then unlocked its energy matrix's seventh energy seal again with a right index finger zing.

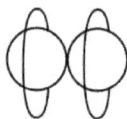

The seventh seal

With this unlocked, Higher Consciousness shouted that "This master force ends my energy fetus' energy labor and deification process. It will be when I have incarnated and deified at least 144,000 first sanctuaries who will become my second sanctuary capstone and ignite it."

With its energy fetus' energy labor complete, Higher

Consciousness unlocked its eighth energy seal from its energy matrix and declared,

"This master force begins my energy fetus energy birth on December 21, 2082."

The eighth seal

It once again hovered over Lucy and thanked her for her forthcoming efforts. Lucy did not need to answer. Her glowing smile said everything. Higher Consciousness glided back to Lucifer and thanked him for watching Lucy complete her role. I noticed Lucifer's response was odd and different from Lucy's. He turned his head away from Higher Consciousness and simply nodded his head up and down.

Higher Consciousness then floated back to the blackboard and using its left and right index fingers released energy zings to open its ninth energy seal on its energy matrix.

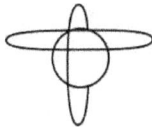

The ninth seal

Higher Consciousness informed Lucy and Lucifer that they could be part of this master force if they choose. It continued to explain that the unlocking of its ninth energy seal from its energy matrix continued its energy fetus' energy birth.

It went back to the blackboard and with its left and right index fingers unleashed its energy zings to unlock its tenth and final energy seal from its energy matrix.

The tenth seal

After directing its tenth master force into its energy womb, Higher Consciousness turned and announced that "This master force closes my energy womb and completes my energy pregnancy."

PART II:
INSIDE THE SECRET

CHAPTER 5

CROSSING THE ENERGY THRESHOLD

I WATCHED AS HIGHER CONSCIOUSNESS handed the locked energy matrix to Lucy. When Lucy held it, she adoringly looked at Higher Consciousness. It was a look of; *Are you really allowing me to hold this?*

When Higher Consciousness nodded, Lucy brought it close to her heart and held it there. She sensed its energy and power. After a moment, she moved it away from her heart, but then quickly brought it back again and closed her eyes. I watched as she held it close to her heart for some time.

When she was finished she handed it back to Higher Consciousness and said, "Thank you."

Higher Consciousness than handed it to Lucifer. Lucifer took it and placed it on his desk. He studied its every detail with great alacrity. When he was done, he thanked Higher Consciousness and handed it back.

Holding the energy matrix, Higher Consciousness floated back to its levitating position above the front counter. From here it held the energy matrix again above its head and proclaimed to Lucy and Lucifer "I grant you authority to complete my energy pregnancy through my master forces. Do not add or subtract anything to them. Lucifer you are my male consciousness whom I grant authority to conceive and gestate my energy fetus. Lucy you are my female consciousness whom I grant authority to deliver and birth my energy fetus. Do either of you have any questions?"

Silence determined its next move.

"When birthed you will both be my Divine Child's consciousness."

Looking at Lucifer, Higher Consciousness asked "Are you ready to begin my energy pregnancy."

Lucifer replied, "Yes."

Looking at Lucy, Higher Consciousness asked, "Are you ready to begin my energy pregnancy?"

Lucy answered, "Yes."

As Higher Consciousness let go of its energy matrix it began to slowly rise and stopped about two feet above Higher Consciousness' outstretched hands.

I watched Lucy and Lucifer gaze intently at the energy matrix. Then Higher Consciousness shouted, "Let it begin!"

As Higher Consciousness unlocked its first energy seal from its energy matrix Lucifer stood up. When he did, Higher Consciousness zinged Lucifer out of the lab's back window—like a bullet shot from a gun leaving vapors behind.

Then Higher Consciousness unlocked its energy matrix's second energy seal and motioned for Lucy to stand up. When she did, Higher Consciousness zinged her out the lab's back window—exactly like Lucifer.

Higher Consciousness' master forces had now begun the energy pregnancy. Lucifer and Lucy were directed along with the first two master forces to their pre-determined positions in the energy womb.

CHAPTER 6

THE ENERGY BETRAYAL

WITH LUCIFER AND LUCY in the energy womb, it was just me and Higher Consciousness left in the lab.

Higher Consciousness floated back to me on the back wall and zinged me that "I needed to die in order to fulfill my life contract. I had gotten off course and am here to unveil my energy pregnancy secret and deification process thoughts"

My guiding light back on Earth was always money. Before my death, I had been uber successful in everything I did. I had created and sold off many businesses; I had the big houses; the fast cars and the hard living to prove it - yet here, none of it mattered.

I remember telling Higher Consciousness, "I don't understand."

Higher Consciousness disclosed, "You are my third eye and must reveal my secret. It is time for my secret's unveiling to begin."

I next watched as Higher Consciousness grew

its third eye out of the top of its head. It was an all-encompassing 360 degree eye. It was Higher Consciousness' "all- seeing eye." Amazingly, whichever way it turned, it emanated its radiance and light of energetic perfection and perfect love.

Higher Consciousness time travelled to now and revealed that Lucy and Lucifer were still in the energy womb.

Lucy had retained her light violet glow, her sanguine smile and her wonderful childlike youth. Lucifer, on the other hand, was almost unrecognizable. His dark violent brilliance I remembered while in the lab was now a reddish, blue and green hue; and his energetic shimmer had become sully and dull. He was now old, haggard had a constant frown and was extremely fragile and frowsy.

I asked Higher Consciousness the obvious, "What happened to Lucifer?

Higher Consciousness answered me by zinging a scene on the blackboard that came to life.

It was the Garden of Eden in all its magnificence. Adam and Eve were playfully enjoying their carefree life. They frolicked around free and careless with huge smiles on their faces. Their love for each other was so genuine: they were clearly Higher Consciousness' first soul mates. They were in "oneness" in every way possible. Multiple times a day they pleasured themselves in an attempt to produce offspring.

The colors of the garden were indescribably brilliant; nothing like I had ever witnessed before in the physical realm. It was the perfect environment; a constant sunlight during the day and an immediate darkness when the sun went down. The temperature didn't change; it was as if it had been set for the pair's ultimate comfort.

Everything was perfect for life's original honeymooners! They had all the food they required, overnight new vegetation would grow for them to eat the next day.

There were numerous species of birds. They came in a variety of colors, shapes and sizes many of which I had never seen before. When they appeared, they would pause if Adam and Eve asked them to. The water around the island was teeming with fish and seafood again the likes I had never seen before. Amazingly, whenever Adam or Eve were hungry, they just had to think about it and fish would jump out of the water and onto the beach for them to eat.

In the middle of the paradise stood Higher Consciousness' tree of knowledge. It was the island's most prominent tree and much larger than any other vegetation. It was colossal and the most perfectly shaped tree I had ever seen.

As I admired the tree, Lucifer sat on one of its lower branches watching Adam and Eve's joyful interactions. Lucifer at this time looked exactly as he did while he was in the lab: youthful with flowing locks of hair; graceful and very handsome.

Then, one day Eve was alone in the garden and approached the tree of knowledge.

Lucifer met her at the base of the tree with a huge piece of fruit in his left hand and gave it to her.

He watched as Eve ate the fruit and give some to Adam, who also ate the fruit.

This produced a huge smile on Lucifer's face. He studied the virginal skin of Adam and Eve and knew exactly where to place his "EGO mark" because Adam and Eve had ate his fruit.

(EGO is an acronym meaning Edging God Out. Its purpose is to deny Higher Consciousness from becoming its Divine Child's energy force at its energy birth. It has also denied mankind of much. It has cut short their life expectancies tremendously. It forced Higher Consciousness to scatter mankind throughout the world. Instead of man living for thousands of years as was Higher Consciousness' original intent, their lives have been drastically curtailed through the ravaging effects of Lucifer's EGO.

EGO has denied Higher Consciousness from completing its deification process to mankind as it fully intended to do 6000 years ago starting with Adam and Eve. EGO has precluded the intimacy, closeness and love that mankind would have already known. EGO has inflicted man with stress, disease, pain and aging. However, most importantly the Luciferian energy of fear and negativity has become the primary energy force of life and mankind.)

When Adam and Eve ate Lucifer's poison, he planted his EGO into their left temples.

Higher Consciousness zinged me that Lucifer plans to become the master energy force of its soon-to-be birthed Divine Child through EGO.

With my question answered, Higher Consciousness again fast-forwarded his third eye to now and revealed that all of mankind is inflicted with Lucifer's left temple EGO implant.

Higher Consciousness then jarred me with its enlightenment that "I died to unveil its energy pregnancy secret and deification process thoughts."

CHAPTER 7

INSIDE OF ENERGY

WHAT HAPPENED NEXT was intoxicating.

I was no longer on the back wall, I was Higher Consciousness' third eye.

When I looked down I saw the top of my head with its light and dark violet shades that became one neutral violet color. In front of me, I saw the two empty desks, previously occupied by Lucy and Lucifer. I looked down on my violet body, hands and arms. At this very moment I was Higher Consciousness.

I was totally lucid and looked deeper into my mind. It was crystal clear, vivid, luminous and oh so blissful! I saw eight of my master forces waiting to be unleashed. They were lined up like sprinters waiting for their race to begin.

I then went inside of my first master force that was in my energy womb. Here I created my first violet atom and first energy cell. With my first atom and cell completed, I created another 100 trillion violet energy atoms and another 100 trillion energy cells. I handed them to Lucifer who was also inside my energy womb and instructed him to place each designated violet energy atom into its designated energy cell so that the cell could protect the atom.

Once Lucifer completed this task, I entered every atom and became their energy essence. As I gazed through the translucence of each atom's protective barrier I witnessed Lucifer on the outside trying to get in.

I went out to Lucifer and told him it was time for him to run an energy cable for me. I connected my energy cable to every atoms' outer protective shield; I handed it to Lucifer and told him to take it back to my lab's window in my energy mind.

Back inside the lab I saw Lucifer arrive. He connected the cable to the lab's window. After he connected the cable, he waved and with a huge grin on his face went back inside my energy womb.

Next, I tested the cable (with myself) in all 100 trillion energy atoms. "Testing... one, two, three; testing... one, two, three." Whenever I heard myself through the cable from within an atom, I confirmed back with my "check."

When every atom's energy sound system was working, I turned my energy sound system on.

I then left my atoms and found Lucy at the top of my energy fetus. I told her that this would be her resting place until I come back to lead her into my energy fetus at the unlocking of my fifth master force. At this moment I pulled a countless amount of angel energy threads out of my all seeing eye and handed them to Lucy and told her to hold them until I return. I then zinged my violet protective barrier between Lucy and Lucifer to keep them separated in my energy womb.

Back in the lab, I unlocked my third energy seal from my energy matrix. With this I re-entered my energy fetus, re-joined Lucifer and zinged my third master force into each of my energy fetus' energy cells. This force directly pulled my energy cells together.

I then moved to an edge of my violet protective barrier where it met my energy womb and zinged my first circular portal in it.

Upon completing my first portal I made a second, similar sized, separate portal in my violet protective barrier directly beside the first portal.

I then moved across my violet protective barrier to its outer edge 180 degrees away from portals one and two. Here I made a third circular portal that was the same size as the first two.

With my first three portals complete, I moved to the exact center point of my violet protective barrier. Here I zinged my fourth and final portal into it. It was much larger than the first three.

Back in the lab I unlocked my energy matrix's fourth energy seal and re-entered my energy fetus to meet Lucifer who was anxiously waiting for my return. This master force authorized my energy atom's atrophy.

With my first four conception and gestation master forces unleashed into my energy womb, I observed Lucifer grow my energy fetus perfectly using their power. Each of my first four master forces grew my energy fetus exactly as I intended and Lucifer oversaw it all.

From the lab I watched Lucifer flawlessly complete my energy fetus' 13.72 billion year gestation adhering to my first four master forces.

CHAPTER 8

SURVIVALIST MAN

HIGHER CONSCIOUSNESS' ENERGY CONCEPTION
and energy gestation was now complete. It was
now time for Lucy to begin her role in the energy
pregnancy.

I saw Lucifer's facial expression change the very
moment I told him to take a break. His eyes sunk into
his head and completely lost his energy and drive
when he realized his role was complete.

When I unleashed my fifth master force I returned to
Lucy at the top of my energy womb. For 13.72 billion
years she did not move or blink while Lucifer was
completing my energy fetus' energy gestation. I told
her it was time for her to transition through my middle
portal directly into my first energy cell. I instructed her
to bring my angel energy threads with her.

When Lucy arrived in our Universe she went directly
into its nucleus which is our planet.

I then unlocked my sixth energy seal from my energy

matrix to begin my energy pregnancy's energy labor through my angel energy threads (that Lucy had).

My angel energy threads purpose is to complete my Divine Child's energy birth through my incarnation into their completed form. My angel energy threads are also the souls of mankind.

I strategically led Lucy to my pre-determined site on Earth and told her to place my designated first angel energy thread on the ground. As she did, I used the ground to form the initial primordial body of the first survivalist man and ignited my angel energy thread to life with my life-force.

My sixth master force's intent for survivalist man was to perfect its physical body form.

As survivalist man was being perfected; Lucifer watched. He watched as Lucy worked directly with me. He watched as each survivalist man reached their life expectancy. He noticed that when they died, their bodies and minds returned into the ground from which they came. He watched their angel energy threads and souls go through the first portal I created in my violet protective barrier.

Lucifer could not see that when my angel energy threads went through my first portal they came back and met with me in my lab. He could not see that I reviewed their life contracts with them and prepared them for their next life experience. He also could not see that I was energetically perfecting their bodies. Once they understood and accepted their life contracts for their next life experience they were sent back to the physical realm through my third portal in my violet protective barrier.

Included with my angel energy threads were the instructions for them to enter their intended pre-destined female. Each angel energy thread was downloaded with my wisdom to either pull their conception switch on or leave if it turned off. Every angel energy thread's determining factor for either turning their conception switch on or leaving it turned off was their energetic calculation I placed in them that instantly evaluated the energetically probability of successfully completing their life contracts purpose through the combined energies of the donor male energy and the mother's female energy. If favorable an angel energy thread would turn on the conception switch and complete their segmentation process that I had instructed them with, if it wasn't, they would leave it off and return back to my divine realm.

To this day, this is how conception either takes place or does not take place.

With my deification of survivalist man's physical body complete, my sixth master force's final intent was ready to be unleashed.

It cleansed the planet through my ice ages. This was completed in order to prepare the ideal physical environment on the planet for my seventh master force to begin.

CHAPTER 9

CONSCIOUSNESS MAN

BACK IN MY LAB, prior to unlocking my seventh master force, I debriefed with my first two consciousness man angel energy threads.

I reviewed, in detail their "life experience contracts" for their forth- coming life experience.

When our debriefing was complete I unlocked my seventh energy seal from my energy matrix to unleash my seventh master force which will complete my energy fetus' energy labor through the deification of consciousness man's mind.

When Eden was prepared my first two consciousness man angel energy threads then exited my lab and went through my third energy portal. They were sent back to Lucy. I instructed Lucy to place my first consciousness man angel energy thread in the middle of Eden's Garden.

Upon Lucy's placement, I once again used the

ground to form the physical body and then brought it to life. It was survivalist man deified male body. My seventh master force intent for consciousness man has always been to deify and energetically perfect them through their mind. Deifying consciousness man's mind is what completes my energy labor.

With my first consciousness man alive I then added his partner: I instructed Lucy to place the second angel energy thread in the first consciousness man. After Lucy's placement, I pulled the angel energy thread out of him; placed it beside him and brought it to life using survivalist man's deified and energetically perfected female body.

Lucy and I watched as Adam and Eve lived carefree in their paradise. However, we both noticed Lucifer lurking off to himself scouting Eden. We noticed he was paying particular attention to the tree of knowledge in the center of the garden. We watched him make himself comfortable on one of its lower hanging limbs. From here Lucifer watched Eve approach.

With Eve at the base of the tree we watched Lucifer jump to the ground and entice her to eat the beautiful fruit he had created. When she did, she unknowingly offered it to Adam. With their bites Lucifer placed his EGO mark in the left temples of both Adam and Eve.

I told Lucy this is Lucifer way to deny my energy pregnancy from happening. If successful he will energetically establish himself as my Divine Child's primary energy force at its energy birth.

From this point on Lucifer's betrayal will deny consciousness man of my existence and pervert life away from me. Because of Lucifer's betrayal I was forced to remove all of my Higher Consciousness energy atoms from the Universe. To this day they still do not exist.

Ever since Lucifer's betrayal he has slowly turned up the intensity of his EGO in consciousness man.

EGO will always renounce me from consciousness man.

Ever since Lucifer's betrayal in Eden, I have helplessly watched him speed up the minds of consciousness man to their present day state of dizziness that has for all intents and purposes removed any and all semblance of me from their minds. He has estranged them from me and made me an alien to them.

Today, in the final microseconds of my Higher Consciousness day, my energy pregnancy secret and deification process thoughts must be revealed to consciousness man so my Divine Child's energy birth can begin on December 21, 2082.

There has never been any force, games, pressure, trouble, stress, pain, duress, intimidation, violence or coercion in me. My seventh energy nature intent has only ever been to complete my energy pregnancy through deifying the minds of consciousness man.

Built into my seventh master force is a safety provision for consciousness man. I cannot incarnate into them and begin my deification process until they authorize me to do so.

After four thousand years of advancing his position Lucifer reached my tipping point of no return. Because of this I was forced to severe him from me.

Since then Lucifer has energetically survived on his own. My life force no longer sustains him. As a result he has aged significantly. He aimlessly wanders and drifts about on his own throughout my energy fetus like a rudderless ship being blown about on the sea.

After severing all energy ties with Lucifer, I immediately replaced my left eye energy and male consciousness. I glorified it as my physical embodiment of what Lucifer was intended to be. As a result my left eye could see again.

Early on, as Jesus began fulfilling my earthly purpose, he met Lucifer in the wilderness where all Lucifer could do was feebly try and persuade Jesus from me. Jesus was not Adam and Eve. This encounter lasted less than a minute and was my initial crowning earthly event through Jesus. My final crowning earthly event through Jesus was his ascension that revealed consciousness man's physical immortality potential. Jesus's Alpha and Omega, first and last, beginning and end crowning earthly events were his most significant. They represent how my deification process for consciousness man begin and end.

Lucifer's betrayal has caused all of consciousness man to miss out on 6000 years of my seventh master force infinite potentials that they were intended to have through my deification into their mind.

The difference between what I intended consciousness man to be by now and what Lucifer has forced consciousness man to endure is the energy chasm that must be cured prior to December 21, 2082.

Curing this energy chasm can only be through my deification process and incarnation into consciousness man that would have already happened 6000 years ago if not for the betrayal of Lucifer.

During every soul's final "between life experience debriefing" I have downloaded my energy password of "deification process" into them. With now revealing my deification process to every final life experience soul it will automatically awaken them from their "in body" slumber placed on them by EGO.

The revealing of my deification process awakens every final life experience soul to unleash their lifelong freedom, purpose and evolution which is to have me incarnate into their body and mind.

My incarnation into the body and mind of consciousness man is every final life experience soul's passion that will unleash its freedom, purpose and evolution.

CHAPTER 10

THE DIVINE CHILD

WHEN I UNLOCK MY EIGHTH ENERGY SEAL on December 21, 2082 at 11:11:11 GMT from my energy matrix, my eighth master force will begin my Divine Child's energy birth.

All of consciousness man who has authorized me to incarnate into them will begin their immortality by ascending physically from the planet.

My eighth master force will instantaneously unshackle their physical world's restraints so their ascension can begin.

These are my first fruits. They are my second sanctuary capstone and will ignite it.

My eighth master force will move the first fruits in a spiraling clockwise direction toward my energy cervix towards the Sun. For 1000 years they will travel where no man has ever gone into every atom within the Universe propelled by my second sanctuaries energy.

Simultaneously, all of my other 100 trillion energy cells will begin their energy birth by also moving through my energy cervix spiraling towards the Sun. When all energy cells have passed through the Sun my Divine Child will be born and my ninth master force will be complete.

The unleashing of my tenth and final master force will conclude my energy pregnancy with the closing of my energy womb.

Part III:
Unveiling the Secret

CHAPTER 11

THE JOURNEY BACK

WHEN I SAW THAT HIGHER CONSCIOUSNESS' Divine Child birth was complete, I suddenly found myself back in the "holy-of-holies."

I knew and felt I was where I needed to be. I had to be part of Higher Consciousness' Divine Child. I knew this was where I was going and I wanted nothing else.

Suddenly, much to my regret, Higher Consciousness' final collective zing informed me that "I must return to unveil my energy pregnancy secret and deification process thoughts."

Higher Consciousness slowly decreased its energetic intensity. Its hexagram fire went out and its six violet colored stars disappeared; finally, its warmth was gone.

This was the exact moment when my soul's passion was unlocked.

I remember exiting the holy-of-holies again through the veil. I was now moving in the opposite direction down the hallway from which I had come. Again I sensed the same force guiding me, I went down the stairway that was now on my right.

At the bottom of the stairway I turned to my right as I was now back on the main level. I exited Higher Consciousness' inner sanctuary doorway that was now on my left. I recall moving slowly through the courtyard. As I approached the great wall that surrounded the courtyard, its large wooden gate automatically opened and I exited through it.

I was being led back to where my journey began. I remember moving up the mountainside and when I reached the mountaintop - I immediately saw a rabbit hole. I knew I needed to go down it and gladly did.

Through the rabbit hole I began transcending through the cosmos of time (this time) in a downward direction.

Suddenly, I was back in the Bella Coola Hospital emergency room. From the top of the room, I remember seeing everybody frantically scrambling about. I saw the doctor, the nurse and a handful of unrecognizable others.

I recall slowly floating down from the emergency room ceiling to the immediate right of where my body rested and after a brief moment, horizontally re-entered it. The very instant I re-entered my body I opened my eyes and looked straight into the doctor's eyes that were directly over me about six inches away.

When I opened my eyes, he calmly said to everybody, "Its okay, he's back."

I remember the doctor stitching up my throat. When the procedure was complete, I remember being wheeled out of the emergency room on the stretcher into my private room.

The hospital staff nicknamed me the "miracle man" for surviving death. They told me I was unresponsive for a couple of minutes; however, everything would be normal because my brain could survive up to six minutes after my heart stopped without any damage. I knew the real miracle was that my brain had internalized everything Higher Consciousness had downloaded me with during my NDE. (Since then, medical experts have told me that because my brain was still alive when I returned from my death it could automatically process what I was zinged during my NDE. To my brain my NDE zings are just another consciousness experience.)

Higher Consciousness' energy pregnancy secret and deification process thoughts were etched into my mind and has remained at the forefront of my consciousness (7/24) ever since I returned from the other side. I just had nature quantified to me from the Source's mouth and I could not sleep with the excitement it generated. I pondered over and over how am I ever going to reveal what I had just been downloaded with. I couldn't stop feeling and sensing the profundity of what had just been revealed.

I constantly wondered how can this wisdom capture the imagination and impact others. I knew I had been downloaded with the answers to life's deepest mysteries that have haunted us forever; yet, I had no idea how to communicate it.

CHAPTER 12

DISCLOSURE

"We shall require a substantially new way of thinking if mankind is to survive."
Albert Einstein (1879 – 1955)

I KNEW THE REASON I SURVIVED death was to unveil Higher Consciousness' energy pregnancy secret and deification process thoughts to fulfill Higher Consciousness' energy pregnancy. By successfully revealing it and awakening all final life experience souls Higher Consciousness' Divine Child and Immortal Infinite can be born on December 21, 2082.

I sensed my NDE downloads needed to create a whole new way of thinking that does not exist. It would need to go beyond our limitations of consciousness and convey Higher Consciousness' energy pregnancy secret and deification process thoughts to birth its Divine Child. It would need to unleash Higher Consciousness' unstoppable momentum through its deification process which lie beyond our consciousness limitations EGO has created.

As I look back on the 20 years since I returned from the afterlife, I can clearly see my afflatus with Higher Consciousness did not end when I returned from my NDE. My NDE was the energetic grounding I needed to establish Higher Consciousness' life potential network that will extinguish all "Luciferin" energy of fear and negativity and replace it with the Higher Consciousness' energetic perfection, perfect love and hope through its deification process.

Back in the physical realm, Higher Consciousness' perspective was constantly revealed for me. During my 20-year Higher Consciousness internship, I was allowed to see and understand energy from the perspective of Higher Consciousness.

It felt like energy was opening up for me to crawl inside of it like I did during my NDE. I was again "one" with energy. I could see how energy either adhered to Higher Consciousness' master forces or repelled against its master forces. I could see if energy was moving toward Higher Consciousness' completion or trying to rewrite the script that cannot work. If I had not died and been zinged with Higher Consciousness' energy pregnancy secret and deification process thoughts, I never would have been able to understand energy from its perspective during my 20-year internship.

Circumstances appeared in many different ways; for example, a conversation or advertising (on a bus or on the radio) but mostly they came from within in the form of intuitive promptings. It was as though I was wearing energy antennas of Higher Consciousness and whenever I needed to interpret its meaning of a life event through energy, they would be turned on so I could.

Another interesting aspect of my internship was that many tried to derail me from it even though they had no idea I was on it.

Very early on in my internship I realized that the existence of a Higher Consciousness is the most polarizing question amongst man today. It has been the subject of hot debate between philosophers, scientist and theologians for the past 2500 years. There are many who sit in the "Yes" camp and believe that such a force exists and many who sit in the "No" camp and don't believe such a force exists. My NDE revealed to me that Higher Consciousness' energy pregnancy secret and deification process thoughts is the missing link that binds all opinions, faiths and beliefs together.

The existence of a Higher Consciousness has never been proven. It's not as though anyone has ever been able to say, "Yep, there's Higher Consciousness."

The more I was impressed with this, the more I realized that we have been trying to solve life's most polarizing question without even knowing what the picture of the puzzle looks like were supposed to put together. The complete picture of Higher Consciousness is its energy pregnancy and deification process. It reveals what it is, how it works, when it happens, why it's happening and most importantly - where it's leading us.

During my NDE, Higher Consciousness zinged me with the realization that energy is simply its second-by-second energetic perfection and perfect love communication that moves every atom in every Universe towards the fulfilling of its energy pregnancy. It is the unseen glue of Higher Consciousness. The energy pregnancy secret and deification process thoughts of Higher Consciousness has been revealed at this time to wake us up and complete Higher Consciousness' energy pregnancy.

My 20 year Higher Consciousness internship revealed how everything in life adheres to the Higher Consciousness' energy pregnancy master forces. It revealed that energy is the end product produced by every atom in the Universe. Energy does not lead us like we have always thought; rather it is the by-product produced by every atom through its master force lead. Without the Higher Consciousness' master force direction to every atom there is no energy as evidenced by when a person dies.

I learned during my 20-year Higher Consciousness internship that the minds of consciousness man through science have done a great job of identifying Higher Consciousness' micro-essence as the driving force of the atom while religion and spritualty has identified Higher Consciousness' macro-aspect as the driving force and highest power that leads the show.

Unfortunately, my 20 year Higher Consciousness internship also revealed countless times that neither religion nor science will ever be any closer to comprehending Higher Consciousness than they are presently at because neither have the picture of Higher Consciousness.

PART IV: QUANTIFYING THE SECRET

CHAPTER THIRTEEN

THE ENERGY CONCEPTION

O

Higher Consciousness' First Energy Seal.

WISDOM ACCEPTS wisdom unconditionally.

Higher Consciousness' wisdom is its master forces that complete its energy pregnancy.

It is the wisdom the soul knows and requires to fulfill.

However, the mind is presently limited to only comprehend the frequencies of knowledge that are logical, tangible and real. Higher Consciousness' frequencies of wisdom are not seen: they are felt. Herein lies the mind's conundrum, how can it accept that which is felt?

EGO denies the mind from accepting the existence of a Higher Consciousness because it does not meet the minds basic requirement of survival.

There are 168 hours in a week; yet, at best even the most faithful spend only a small amount of time in their daily communications with their God. Why? Because there has never been a moment in a person's daily devotional life that earns a living or puts food on the table. Time with God lacks the means to practically sustain one's survival needs and because of this EGO has easily been able to keep the existence of a Higher Consciousness away from the mind.

What if Higher Consciousness could fulfill your survival needs beyond anything you could ever imagine? Would this open your mind up to looking into the possible existence of a Higher Consciousness? Due to Lucifer's betrayal this is exactly what Higher Consciousness was forced to do.

To the mind, Higher Consciousness has been made to appear insignificant and irrelevant because it has nothing to do with your daily survival requirements. To the mind there is a huge disconnect between a Higher Consciousness and your survival needs.

How could any mind possibly accept a Higher Consciousness if it has no relevance in your day-to-day survival? It can't.

To the mind Higher Consciousness is either some distant, mystical, abstract presence that has no logical relevance in your survival or some inner feeling that somehow is meant to enhance your daily survival while completely lacking the practical application to do so. Neither option generates the logic your mind requires for survival.

Ever since returning from my NDE I realized that Higher Consciousness' monetary potential is the minds portal to accept its existence as it far exceeds anything our consciousness's limitations has ever shown.

For Higher Consciousness' to unleash it's monetary potential your mind must first accept it can do so. This begins with the understanding of what it can do? Why it must be revealed now? And most importantly how it will affect you in your life?

It took me 20 years to unearth the Higher Consciousness' energy pregnancy "life proofs" so the mind could consider what I was zinged during my NDE.

The first master force of Higher Consciousness was its conception. Its life proofs are what happened when time began.

During my NDE, I became Higher Consciousness and went inside of its first master force to reveal its slow motion, frame-by-frame energetic happenings that were taking place as it was unleashed. It was a glimpse into what was happening on the inside of the Big Bang and Creations first second of existence.

Science's calculations have estimated Higher Consciousness' first master force was unleashed approximately 13.75 billion years ago to create the singularity.

It was the Belgian physics professor and priest Georges Lemaitre (1894-1966) who in 1927 first theorized the Big Bang. Lemaitre realized the Universe was constantly expanding from its infinitely small, dense, starting point that astrophysicists call the singularity. The singularity was the result of Higher Consciousness' first master force. Two years later, in 1929, it was confirmed by Harvard astronomer Edwin Hubble that the Big Bang was scientifically probable.

It is the exact moment in time that the limitations of consciousness will never be able to grasp because its fundamental laws of physics have no mathematical calculations for creating something out of nothing. However, science, religion, philosophy and spirituality all agree that the Big Bang and Creations zero point came from a colossal amount of energy. Higher Consciousness' subatomic fireworks, science's Big Bang's singularity and religions Creation happened because of the unleashing of Higher Consciousness' first master force which conceived its energy fetus.

Approximately 2500 years ago the Greek philosopher Democritus (460BC–370BC) first theorized about Higher Consciousness' original building blocks – the atom as being an indivisible state of matter. He named the indivisible state of matter Atomos meaning "not to cut."

For over 2000 years Democritus' Atomos Theory was dormant until the English chemist John Dalton (1766-1844) expanded on it. His atomic theory postulated all matter was made up of atoms. Dalton's atomic theory quickly became the theoretical foundation of chemistry.

Over the last 120 years science has developed Dalton's theory further.

In 1897 Sir Joseph John Thompson (1856-1940) totally changed the atom's perspective by discovering the electron.

In 1911 Ernest Rutherford (1871-1937) discovered the atom's nucleus.

In 1913 Neils Bohr (1885-1962) proposed that electrons orbit around the nucleus did not lose energy.

In 1932 James Chadwick (1891-1974) identified the neutron, a particle with mass but no charge.

In 1964 physicists Murray Gell-Mann (b.1929) and George Zweig (b.1937) independently proposed the atom's fundamental constituent and elementary particle is the quark.

However, prior to the 1970s, science had no clue how the atom was held together. It was the discovery of the quark that revealed the atom is subatomically held together by six quarks, which are bound together to form what science calls its strong force of nature.

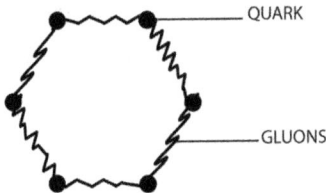

The atoms subatomic structure strong force of nature gluons and quarks.

Thanks to science Democritus' 2500 year old theory of the Atomos has been proven right down to the energetic six quark hexagram and strong force of nature red, green and blue gluons that hold the atom together.

To understand just how infinitesimal the atom is, a person weighing 70kg is estimated to have 7,000,000,000,000,000,000,000,000,000 atoms in their body. Sciences present calculations estimate that there are approximately one septenvigintillion, 1,000,000,000,000,000,000,000,000,000,000,000,000,000,000,000,000,000,000,000,000,000,000,000,000,000,000,000 atoms in the Universe.

Science has proven that the atom's subatomic strong force of nature is about 100 times stronger than the electromagnetic force and orders of magnitude stronger than gravity. This strong force of nature's red, green and blue gluon particle colors has no effect outside the atom's nucleus. Science has also proven that the strong nuclear force is the essence of every atom and unknowingly they identified Higher Consciousness micro essence that is in every atom.

Higher Consciousness is both a macro essence that resides in its energy mind (whom I met during my NDE) and a micro essence of six quarks and strong nuclear force that resides subatomically in every atom in its energy womb.

CHAPTER 14

CONTINUING THE ENERGY CONCEPTION

BY BEING INSIDE OF Higher Consciousness' first master force it revealed that the Big Bang and Creations first second did so much more than simply establishing itself as the atoms six quarks and strong nuclear force essence.

It also produced an additional 100 trillion energy atoms and established its energetic pathways.

Today the existence of Higher Consciousness 100 trillion energy atoms has evolved into one of science's newest frontiers. It is the frontier of Parallel Universe potentiality.

Science's Parallel Universe theory is in its infancy. It hypothesis' that Parallel Universes are alternate worlds that interact and constantly influence one another. It further hypothesis' that instead of a collapse in which quantum particles choose to occupy one state or another, they actually exist simultaneously in all states.

If time permitted, one day science would eventually discover that Higher Consciousness has left wormholes between Universes that would confirm a Parallel Universe connectivity of which is the energy fetus' connectivity.

During Higher Consciousness' first second of life, it also produced an energy meta-system of vertical and horizontal communications pathways that science theoretically refers to as "entanglement and superstring."

Entanglement is science's attempt to explain how two particles can be the same quantum state and not individual quantum states; thus, the term entangled. From the perspective of Higher Consciousness life is simply one huge entanglement of particle intertwining in the same state within its energy womb.

Albert Einstein believed all attempts to explain entanglement were flawed because he did not agree that particles could affect one another faster than the speed of light. To take his reasoning one step further, the crux of what Einstein was really saying is he believed Higher Consciousness works at the speed of light. He went on to describe entanglement as "spooky action at a distance" and denied quantum mechanics as an incomplete picture. He further believed that someday in the future its "extra hidden variables" would be made known.

To date science have been unable to discover any hidden variables that Einstein was referring to and they never will. They are what occurred before the beginning of time, again, where the limitations of consciousness cannot go. However your soul knows it well.

The Big Bang's singularity first second established Higher Consciousness' two energy communication pathways for its energy fetus.

Its first energy fetus energy communication pathway is its energetic vertical connection between its macro energy mind and its micro energy mind in every one of its atoms in our Universe and all of its other 100 trillion energy cells.

Its second energy fetus energy communication pathway is its energetic horizontal connection of its micro energy mind with itself in every atom in not only our Universe but also in all of its other 100 trillion energy cells.

These energy communication pathways are science's "entanglement."

Superstring is science's attempt to explain how the particles in Higher Consciousness' vertical communication pathway act as vibrations of tiny super symmetric strings.

Superstring is science's attempt at quantifying the individual particles of Higher Consciousness' vertical communication pathway. What our consciousness limitations will never know is each particles Higher Consciousness energetic pre-determined valuation attached to it. This is so Higher Consciousness can instantly fix any potential particle energy communication glitch were it to happen.

Again, no formula will ever be able to calculate Higher Consciousness' subatomic fireworks of entanglement or superstring because it is where consciousness cannot go. Consciousness simply cannot calculate the formula of creating something from nothing.

Higher Consciousness' first master force of the Big Bang and Creations first second of time was its most profound because while simultaneously conceiving itself it needed to put in place its energy communication foundations for its 100 trillion energy cells so that its energy birth could be completed.

This is where physics meets philosophy.

Religion has also revealed aspects of Higher Consciousness. Approximately 4000 years ago the Star of David, (known in Hebrew as the Shield of David) became the symbol of Judaism. It is the hexagram shape essence that Higher Consciousness is.

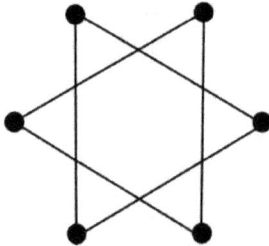

The Star of David symbolizes the perfect state of balance between man and God.

Judaism's Star of David and science's strong nuclear force are both Higher Consciousness' hexagram self. Science has discovered its outside circumference relevance as the essence of every atom.

Religion through Judaism has been shown the inside

relevance of its six star hexagram points. They make up triangular mirror images that represent the perfect state of balance between man and God that must occur to complete the seventh master force and birth Higher Consciousness' Divine Child.

CHAPTER 15

BEGINNING THE ENERGY GESTATION

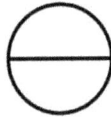

Higher Consciousness' Second Energy Seal.

WITH HIGHER CONSCIOUSNESS' STRONG nuclear force, superstring, entanglement and parallel Universe foundation laid during the first second of its existence, its energy fetus conception was complete.

Higher Consciousness next unlocked its second master force which began its energy fetus' gestation. It was Higher Consciousness' second-second of subatomic fireworks that happened 13.75 billion years ago within its energy womb.

When Higher Consciousness unlocked its second energy seal from its energy matrix, it directed its second master force to come out of its energy matrix.

During my NDE I watched as protons and neutrons began to bind themselves together to form their nucleus in every atom. I watched as Higher Consciousness' energy fetus initial growth happened as the nucleus of every atom was being formed.

I next watched as Higher Consciousness turned and zinged each of its 100 trillion energy fetus atoms with its second master force. Its second master force authorized all its atoms to bind together and form its energy fetus.

I watched as its 100 trillion energy atoms physically began moving toward each other. As they did, they started releasing energy sparks that created colors ranging from violet to blue, to green, to orange to red. These energy sparks connected and grew the energy fetus ever so slightly.

When completed Higher Consciousness added the protective violet barrier to keep Lucy and Lucifer separated in the energy womb.

Higher Consciousness' second master force has been identified by science as the electromagnetic force of nature.

CHAPTER 16

CONTINUING THE ENERGY GESTATION

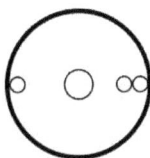

Higher Consciousness' Third Energy Seal.

HIGHER CONSCIOUSNESS' THIRD MASTER force continued its energy fetus' gestation and was released during the Big Bangs and Creations third second of existence.

This master force is the energy fetus' energy instructions that authorized its future continued growth.

During my NDE I held the third violet master force with my left hand and zinged it into the energy fetus' 100 trillion atoms.

I watched as the energy atoms created energy

clusters by pulling themselves together to ultimately form one synchronistic cohesive unit. Their violet, blue, green, yellow, orange and red shades instantly increased their energy intensity to form the cohesive violet color energy fetus.

The third master force has been identified by science as its third fundamental of nature: gravity.

In the 1980s many physicists postulated about a fifth force of nature that was linked with "hypercharge" which in particle physics is a quantum number relating to strong interactions.

What physicists confirmed in the 1980s was that this mystical fifth force was roughly the strength of gravity and had a range of anywhere from less than a millimeter to cosmological scales.

Science has been unable to duplicate the results of their original experiments and they never will. Why? Because it is the gravitational force of the soul. Higher Consciousness' third master force pulls the soul through its first and second portals.

Souls are Higher Consciousness' angel energy threads that came out of its third eye and were handed to Lucy at the release of its second master force. Like Higher Consciousness, they are immortal and never die. When a body dies they enter into sciences fifth fundamental to exit the physical tangible realm and enter Higher Consciousness' divine intangible realm through the first circular portal.

Higher Consciousness' divine realm is its energy mind. Here it debriefs with its returned angel energy threads and zings them with their next life experience purpose and life contract. When a soul agrees to fulfill their next life contract and life experience purpose, they exit the divine realm through the third circular portal to re-enter the physical realm.

When the soul re-enters the physical realm, they move directly to their predestined female terminus. During their debriefing Higher Consciousness downloads every soul with the female they are to enter into as they re-enter the physical realm. When entering their pre-destined female, souls energetically burrow themselves into the predestined female terminus hypothalamus.

The hypothalamus is the portion of the brain, which contains a number of small nuclei, which have a variety of functions. The hypothalamus triggers the anterior lobe of the pituitary gland to release the follicle-stimulating hormone, which produces the female's ovulation.

After ovulation and intimacy the soul's wisdom will either accept or deny conception based upon its predetermined life experience purpose from their life contract that was downloaded by Higher Consciousness during their between life debriefing. If the energetic circumstances are favorable for the soul to carry out its life experiences predetermined purpose, conception takes place. If the energetic circumstances are not favorable for the soul to carry out its life energy contract's predetermined purpose, the soul (based on the woman and man's combined energies) will not authorize conception to occur.

It is impossible for the fields of mathematics, probability and statistics to calculate the chances of every single person who has ever walked the face of the Earth to have (for the most part) the same 100 trillion cells. It is not a random chance that this has happened. It happens because at conception every soul energetically transcends into the ovum of their future mother to carry out Higher Consciousness' life experience instructions for the segmentation process to fully develop the fetus until its birth.

When the fetus is fully developed by way of Higher Consciousness' energy instructions, the fetus and soul are birthed in the physical realm.

As a soul exits the body during a NDE, they also transition out of the physical realm through the second circular portal back into Higher Consciousness' divine realm.

They also debrief with Higher Consciousness whereby they are put back on track to fulfill their life contract purpose. When Higher Consciousness re-acquaints them with their life purpose, they are sent back into the physical realm to complete their soul's life contract.

CHAPTER 17

COMPLETING THE ENERGY GESTATION

Higher Consciousness' Fourth Energy Seal.

HIGHER CONSCIOUSNESS' FOURTH MASTER force
was put in place during the Big Bangs and Creations
fourth second of existence 13.75 billion years ago. It is
the energy that ends the energy fetus' gestation.

Higher Consciousness' fourth master force is its
force that atrophies and decays.

Science coins this master force as the weak force of
nature. It was first theorized in 1933 by Enrico Fermi.
It is best described as a non-contact force field with
a very short finite range that causes neutron decay
within the atom.

Through science it has been quantified as the reason that initiates supernovas. (A supernova is an astronomical event that occurs during the last stellar evolutionary stages of a massive stars life.) It is marked by one final titanic explosion similar to life's initial explosion that happened at the Big Bang. However, a supernova is only a fraction of the strength of what the Big Bang and Creation was.

The limitations of consciousness has no clue that Higher Consciousness has been testing supernovas within the physical realm of its energy womb in far off regions because of Lucifer's betrayal. Its purpose is to evaluate the efficacy of its fourth master force on the Universe's atoms in case it needs to activate this process in our Universe if Lucifer's betrayal cannot be overcome.

The first recorded supernova was recorded in 185 AD by Chinese astronomers. The brightest supernova was recorded in 1006 AD. It was recorded by both Chinese and Islamic astronomers. It was the brightest because it was the closest one Higher Consciousness implemented to consciousness man.

Supernovas reveal the spectacular atomic color atoms achieved during Higher Consciousness' gestation of its energy fetus. The limitations of consciousness also does not know that Supernovas are the inverse energy reaction that Higher Consciousness would use to unwind and destroy our Universe in its totality if Lucifer's betrayal and energy of fear and negativity cannot be overcome by December 21, 2082.

The Big Bang and Creation reached their zenith three seconds after being conceived. From here the energy fetus began to cool and grow under the direction of Higher Consciousness' gestation master force directives.

During Higher Consciousness' 13.75 billion year energy pregnancy (that ends when its Divine Child's energy birth begins on December 21, 2082) its gestational master force's two through four have constantly produced atoms in all one hundred trillion energy cells. This is how and why Higher Consciousness' energy fetus has grown to its infinite size today.

Our Universe is Higher Consciousness' most important and lead energy cell within its energy fetus.

CHAPTER 18

THE ENERGY BREAKING OF WATER

Higher Consciousness' Fifth Energy Seal.

AFTER GESTATING for 13.72 billion years it was now time for Higher Consciousness to begin its energy labor.

It began 3.2 million years ago when it unlocked its fifth master force from its energy matrix.

At this moment its energy womb was fully stretched because of the size its 100 trillion energy cell energy fetus had grown to.

For 13.72 billion years Lucy was outside of the energy fetus within Higher Consciousness' energy womb and watched its gestation and growth. With its fifth master force unleashed Higher Consciousness returned to Lucy at the top of its energy womb.

It instructed Lucy to now move through the middle portal with all of its angelic energy life threads and enter its first cell's nucleus, which is our planet.

From here Higher Consciousness led Lucy to its pre-destined point of empowerment on Earth.

With Higher Consciousness' breaking of water master force unleashed, Lucifer's 13.72 billion year conception and gestation duties were complete and Lucy's energy role began.

CHAPTER 19

SURVIVALIST MAN – BEGINNING THE ENERGY LABOR

Higher Consciousness' Sixth Energy Seal.

THE UNLEASHING OF HIGHER Consciousness' sixth master force happened one second after the unleashing of its fifth master force 3.2 million years ago. The intent of this master force unleashing was to begin the energy fetus' labor and deification process.

With Lucy at her point of empowerment on Earth, Higher Consciousness had already selected its first angelic life thread to begin its energy fetus' energy labor. Its anointed point of empowerment on Earth was its most glorious location on the planet at that time. It is today known as Ethiopia.

Higher Consciousness instructed Lucy to place the chosen angelic life thread on the ground. As she did, Higher Consciousness grabbed the dirt from the ground and molded its initial primordial body around it. When complete Higher Consciousness breathed its life-force into it. This became mankind's first living being that ironically has come to be known as Lucy.

Survivalist man was born and energetically consisted of three components: a body, a mind and a soul. Like consciousness man today, the soul was survivalist man's most powerful component as without it the body and mind cannot live. During conception, souls establish the strong nuclear force into every atom.

Every soul's energetic anatomy consists of two parts: its soul body and its soul mind. The soul's mind is also the minds collective unconsciousness. It's where the wisdom of Higher Consciousness is located while the soul's body resides in our spine.

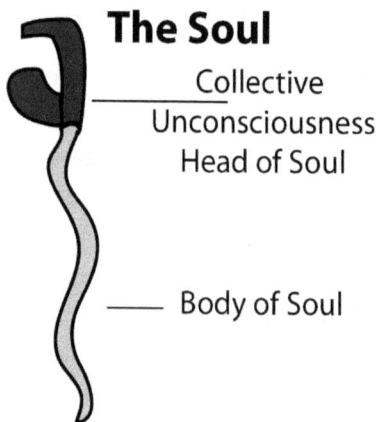

The Soul

Collective
Unconsciousness
Head of Soul

—— Body of Soul

Our soul mind is our minds collective unconsciousness and physiologically is our brainstem. Higher Consciousness purposely limited survivalist man's energetic traits of security, sexuality, and spirituality because this was not survivalist man's primary need.

The body of survivalist man's soul (like our souls today) ran through its spinal cords central canal. The central canal of survivalist man's spinal cord ran longitudinally through the length of its entire spinal cord. As it is today, it was filled with cerebrospinal fluid (CSF). CSF is a clear colorless bodily fluid whose main purpose is to create a natural buoyancy for the brain. It allows the brain not to be impaired by its own weight that would have choked off survivalist man's blood supply and immediately killed it. It also protected survivalist man's brain tissue from injury and provided a chemical stability for the brain.

Central Canal of Spinal Cord

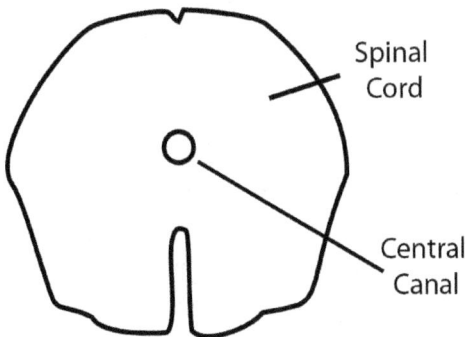

The body of the soul runs longitudinally through the spinal cord's central canal.

Higher Consciousness' sixth master force's intent was to energetically perfect the bodies of survivalist man through its deification process which it did when the soul returned to the divine realm after completing a life experience.

For nearly 3.2 million years Higher Consciousness energetically perfected the bodies of survivalist man through its deification process in the divine realm. Lucifer watched as Lucy worked directly with Higher Consciousness through the release of the angel life threads it had given Lucy 13.72 billion years earlier.

Lucifer took particular notice when survivalist man died after fulfilling their life experience and their body and minds turned back to dust. He watched their souls leave their bodies after their bodies died. He watched as the soul exited the physical realm through the first portal Higher Consciousness created in its violet protective barrier during the unleashing of its third master force 13.72 billion years earlier.

Once a soul transcended out of the physical realm Lucifer did not know that they went back and debriefed with Higher Consciousness. Lucifer also did not know that Higher Consciousness was deifying the soul for its next life experience.

Its sixth master force deified the bodies of survivalist man after 3.2 million years of soul life experiences.

Over the 3.2 million years, survivalist man evolved from tree dwellers to upright walkers. As the bodies of survivalist man evolved they did so by evolving forward. As Higher Consciousness' evolved survivalist man they began to climb down from trees to the ground primarily because over the years their climate changed from a lush forest to a dry grassland.

To deify the bodies of survivalist man Higher Consciousness needed to expand survivalist man into other climates of the world (other than Ethiopia). It first expanded survivalist man to other regions in Africa that we know today as Chad, Kenya, Tanzania, Malawi and South Africa.

Later, it placed survivalist man in other climates beginning with modern day Georgia (on the Black Sea south of Russia) followed by modern day China, Indonesia, Turkey and Spain. It was an effort to deify and energetically perfect survivalist man's body in all climatic circumstances. The first remains of survivalist man appeared in North America a mere 13,000 years ago.

As survivalist man's bodies deified and attained their energetic perfection, Higher Consciousness began to energetically cleanse the planet in order to complete its sixth master force.

For the last one million years of its sixth master force, Higher Consciousness energetically cleansed the planet through various ice ages beginning in Earth's northern hemisphere. This was its sixth master force's final intent.

Its last ice age reached its climax about 20,000 years ago. At this time it began to melt away. Its final sixth master force ice age was completed approximately 10,000 years ago.

With the planet cleansed and purified Higher Consciousness was now ready to unlock its seventh master force from its energy matrix.

CHAPTER 20

CONSCIOUSNESS MAN – COMPLETING THE ENERGY LABOR

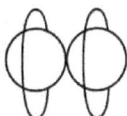

Higher Consciousness' Seventh Energy Seal.

HIGHER CONSCIOUSNESS' MOST CRITICAL stage of its energy pregnancy began approximately 6000 years ago.

It began when it unleashed its seventh master force out of its energy mind through its energy matrix into its energy womb.

The intent of its seventh master force is to complete its energy labor and complete its deification of mankind so its Divine Child can begin its energy birth.

Lucifer had watched from the sidelines as Lucy

and Higher Consciousness prepared Earth for the arrival of consciousness man. He watched as Higher Consciousness completed its utopian paradise after the last ice age melted.

Higher Consciousness cleansed Earth in order to cultivate and manicure Eden into its pre-destined energetic perfection and perfect love ideal energy nirvana.

When Eden was fully prepared, Higher Consciousness instructed Lucy to place its first consciousness man angel life thread on the ground in the middle of Eden.

With consciousness man's first angel life thread on the ground, Higher Consciousness once again took dirt from the ground and molded its energetically perfected and deified survivalist man male body around its first consciousness man angel life thread. When complete, it once again breathed its life-force into its perfected male form. Its first energetically perfected male consciousness man has come to be known as Adam.

With Adam perfected and living in his utopian paradise, Higher Consciousness had him fall asleep. While he slept Lucy placed Higher Consciousness' next consciousness man angel life thread inside of him. Then, Higher Consciousness reached inside and pulled its second consciousness man angel life thread out of Adam and laid it on the ground beside him. Here it molded its energetically perfected survivalist female body around its angel life thread. When complete, once again it breathed its life-force into the energetically perfected and deified female form. Its first consciousness man female has come to be known as Eve.

Over survivalist man's 3.2 million-year period, Higher Consciousness completed its sixth master force by energetically perfecting and deifying the male and female bodies of survivalist man.

It was now time for the seventh master force to energetically perfect and deify consciousness man's mind so that Higher Consciousness' energy labor could be completed for its December 21, 2082 Divine Child birth to begin.

To do so the minds of consciousness man must be energetically perfected and deified as survivalist man's body was during the sixth master force.

The intent of Higher Consciousness' seventh master force is for the minds of consciousness man to be the energetic perfection and perfect love that Higher Consciousness is.

When the minds of consciousness man have been deified mankind will become Higher Consciousness' first sanctuary.

Higher Consciousness designed consciousness man's mind with a consciousness, a sub-consciousness and an unconsciousness.

Within the unconsciousness lies the collective unconsciousness. It is the wisdom of and energetic essence of both the mind and the soul.

The Energetic Mind

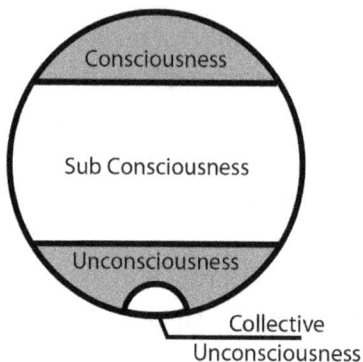

Higher Consciousness designed the consciousness of consciousness man's mind to be its energetic storage facility that receives and sends energetic signals. Consciousness was designed to receive energetic signals from one of two directions: either externally from external stimuli or internally from its subconscious, unconsciousness and collective unconsciousness internal stimuli.

ENERGY – THOUGHTS – ACTIONS:

Today the mind's energetic stimuli can be measured through brain waves. Brain waves are measured by electroencephalography (EEG). EEG records electrical activity along the scalp. It measures voltage fluctuations, which result from ionic current flows within the neurons of the brain.

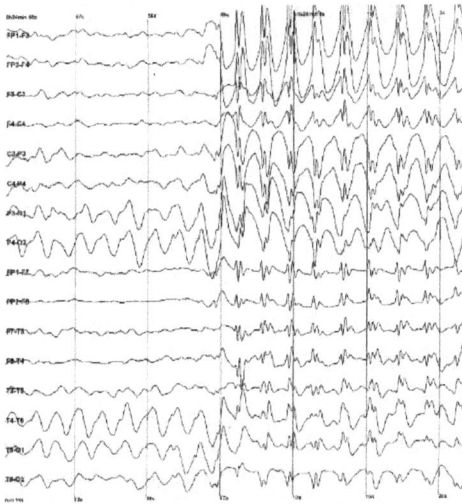

EEG Recording of scalp's Electrical Activity

Left-brained dominance indicates a person resonates more with their external stimuli.

Right-brained dominance indicates a person resonates more with their internal stimuli.

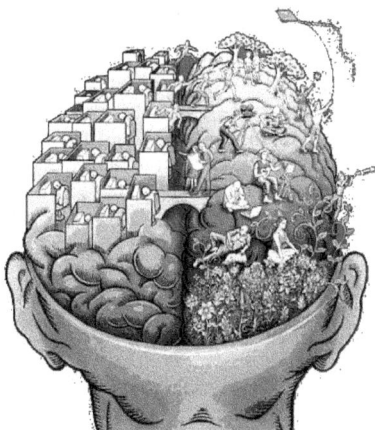

Left and Right Brain Thinking.

Left-brained people are rational. They respond well to verbal instructions. They use logic to solve problems. They look at things sequentially. They measure differences. They are planned, structured and organized. They prefer established proven information. They prefer multiple-choice questions. They control their feelings. They prefer ranked authority structures. They draw on previously accumulated, organized information. They prefer indoor activities. They are detail oriented—facts rule oriented. They are also present and past oriented. They prefer the safe course of action. Their soul age makes up the younger ages of the soul age bell curve.

Left-brained people assume vocations such as computer programmers, technicians, engineers, stockbrokers, scientists, accountants, bookkeepers, human resource directors, administrative assistants, lawyers, doctors, bankers and anything to do with finance.

In contrast, right-brained people are intuitive. They solve problems using their intuition and hunches. They respond to demonstrated instructions. They look for patterns and configurations. They look for similarities, are fluid and spontaneous. They prefer elusive, uncertain information and open-ended questions. They prefer drawing. They are free spirits and prefer outdoor activities. Right- brainers use feelings in making decisions. They are focused on the "big picture." They are present and future oriented. They prefer philosophy, religion and spiritual issues. They are impetuous action takers and risk takers. Their soul age makes up the older ages of the soul age bell curve.

Right-brained people assume vocations, which involve working with people such as counseling and psychology, where they help solve problems. They are artists, musicians, authors, recreational directors and marketing experts. They hold most of the jobs in retail that deal with other people. They are interior designers, hospitality, hotel workers and sales professionals.

Six thousand years ago when Higher Consciousness' seventh master force was unleashed it also began the energetic dilation of its energy cervix. Its energy cervix is the Sun, which is what its Divine Child will be birthed through. As the Sun began to dilate and increase in size, it created the phenomenon we know today as "global warming."

CHAPTER 21

LUCIFER'S BETRAYAL

EVER SINCE LUCIFER LEFT Higher Consciousness'
lab and energy mind to enter the energy womb, he
faithfully performed Higher Consciousness' energetic
perfection and perfect love master force instructions
flawlessly.

He continued to be Higher Consciousness'
perfect reflection as he watched Lucy and Higher
Consciousness work together for 3.2 million years as
Higher Consciousness completed its sixth master force
intent and deification of survivalist man's body.

Higher Consciousness' energy pregnancy was
on schedule for its Divine Child's December 21,
2082 energy birth to begin. Everything had been
energetically perfected exactly as Higher Consciousness
had envisioned. Now, in the final micro-seconds of its
energy day, Lucifer remained in perfect unison and one
with Higher Consciousness.

However, beneath the surface Lucifer's thoughts
did not correlate with his actions. He always felt he

deserved to be the one who should benefit most from the Divine Child's birth. He believed that his 13.72 billion year labor justified him to be the energy fetus' true evolving icon and master. He was always exhilarated by his work, but what really drove him was his desire for power and control. He felt entitled to be the rightful heir of the soon to be birthed Divine Child.

He knew his only opportunity to seize control of the energy pregnancy and become its heir was at the unlocking of Higher Consciousness' seventh master force. Through his insecurities and arrogance he felt he needed to be the most esteemed. For Lucifer being second was not enough, he had to be number one.

He knew his ultimate power and guarantee of privacy would only be when he became Higher Consciousness. There could be no energetic perfection and perfect love of Higher Consciousness on his Divine Child. There could be no 7.5 billion angel energy threads and souls on his Divine Child. Lucifer desired Higher Consciousness' Divine Child to be his private domain of eternal bliss.

His billions of years planning to become Higher Consciousness would soon be crystalized. It would be so easy. He knew everything about the energy pregnancy because he was Higher Consciousness' left eye energy. He knew all he had to do was wait for the seventh master force to be unleashed into the energy womb: then he could pounce. He knew his plan would easily hack into Higher Consciousness' energy pregnancy and plunge his energy dagger deep into its best-laid plans. He knew his plan guaranteed that the Divine Child would be his.

Second-by-second Lucifer felt his destiny approach...
"Soon I will be the forever, soon I will be so much
more than what I have been made to be." After 13.75
billion years of intense planning, he was ready to act.

Higher Consciousness knew if Lucifer was ever
going to interfere with the energy pregnancy it could
only be when its seventh master force was unleashed.

Higher Consciousness knew when Lucifer was
spotted on the tree of knowledge in the Garden of Eden
that he was about to make his move.

Back in the lab prior to commencing their
consciousness man life experience Adam and Eve were
warned of a potential forthcoming attack. This was
why Higher Consciousness warned them to not eat
from the tree of knowledge.

Lucifer anxiously anticipated Eve as she innocently
approached the tree of knowledge. The moment that
Lucifer had forever dreamed about was about to
happen. He had rehearsed the scene over and over again
in his mind and knew exactly what he needed to do.

He appeared to Eve in the energy form that he was,
he didn't have any legs and he simply slithered along
the ground to within inches of her. He knew Higher
Consciousness was watching and he didn't care. He
had meticulously rehearsed his "zugzwang" move.

He confidently asked Eve his brilliant question. He
knew she was programmed to respond honesty. Had
Eve refrained from responding to Lucifer, none of what
was about to happen would have happened and Higher
Consciousness' final micro-seconds of its energy day
would have gone off without a hitch; however, she
answered.

Lucifer knew victory was his the moment Eve responded. He knew his next statement was his most important as he had to convince Eve to eat his fruit, which he easily did. Then came Lucifer's closing argument: he knew Eve did not have the ability to refute. The key buzzwords spoken by Lucifer were about knowing good and evil. However, Lucifer's craftiness added a twist that Eve's mind couldn't process. Lucifer knew what he said was a true statement because for 3.2 million years he had watched the bodies of survivalist man turn to dust and their souls carry on eternally. Lucifer knew Eve's soul was eternal.

Lucifer went back to his perch on the tree of knowledge. From there he watched his plan hatch. He saw Eve carefully examine his fruit. She didn't have a problem with how it looked; it appeared to be agreeable and appealing. In Eve's consciousness limitations she reasoned that by eating it she would be like God. What could be wrong with that? This was great because she would gain the knowledge of God. She took a bite and naturally wanted to share with Adam and gave the fruit to him.

Lucifer was now giddy with excitement because his plan could be fulfilled. It was so much easier than he ever thought. What did he ever have to worry about? Every negative circumstance and reply he had ever envisioned didn't happen. It was so easy.

Lucifer had seamlessly become the driving force of the minds of consciousness man and through Adam and Eve's foolishness there was nothing Higher Consciousness could do about it. The mind was Lucifer's. He could now easily deny the minds of consciousness man any and all connection to Higher Consciousness. Because they ate his fruit, he strategically placed his EGO (Edging God Out) energy blocking software into their left temples.

Lucifer knew that consciousness man's analytic, logic and reasoning resided on the left side of the brain. He knew that by placing his energetic blocking software on consciousness man's left temple he could control and limit the analytic, logic and reasoning of the minds of consciousness man. He could now do anything he pleased.

Adam and Eve authorized Lucifer into them by eating his fruit and disobeying Higher Consciousness. Energetically, they had unknowingly given Lucifer the carte blanche freedom he needed to control and limit all minds of consciousness man.

Lucifer is consciousness man's energetic surgeon who has energetically implanted his blocking energy software that only tunes into his energy of fear and negativity by creating doubt and insecurity to limit and control consciousness.

Now it is nothing more than a waiting game.

CHAPTER 22

LUCIFER'S EGO

LUCIFER NOW HAD *carte blanche* authority to implant his EGO into the minds of all of consciousness man because of Adam and Eve's blunder.

He controlled the fear and negativity energy frequencies through his EGO and declared himself: the authority of man. He was successful in hijacking the minds of consciousness man away from Higher Consciousness through his energetic implant. He knows he will be victorious by simply creating doubt and insecurity in the minds of consciousness man. By doing so, his fear and negativity energy would limit and control consciousness man to whatever way best served his interest.

For 6000 years, Lucifer has been mankind's energetic prefrontal lobotomy surgeon. He has performed countless energy surgeries and inserted his EGO chip on the left temples of everyone who has ever lived over the past 6000 years.

This is why doubt and insecurity exists and it is why

his Luciferin energy frequencies of fear and negativity have become the dominant energy force in life for the last 6000 years.

The pentagram is Lucifer's EGO chip that has been implanted in the left temples of consciousness man.

Lucifer's EGO chip is an energetic inverted pentagram. It represents Lucifer's carnal energy of fear and negativity that is activated by doubt and insecurity. With one point down rather than two as on Higher Consciousness's hexagram, Lucifer has made a copycat symbol of Higher Consciousness. It is how Lucifer blocks the minds of consciousness man from Higher Consciousness. EGO authorizes only the energy of Lucifer into the mind. EGO is the accepted symbol of Occultism, Satanism and Freemasonry.

What a brilliant plan Lucifer hatched: control the mind of consciousness man and Higher Consciousness' final frontier so victory is his. Lucifer has controlled the minds of consciousness man for 6000 years by eliminating all direct transmissions and communications with Higher Consciousness. Lucifer is consciousness man's only energy force. He will only allow in the frequencies of knowledge he wants a particular mind to have.

EGO is Lucifer's portal to becoming Higher Consciousness. With it he controls the outcome of the energy pregnancy. Higher Consciousness' seventh master force intent for the mind of consciousness man cannot be heard because of Lucifer's EGO. It has turned consciousness man into misguided sheep, who lack the wisdoms of Higher Consciousness.

Since Eve, no one has been exempt from Lucifer's EGO. As a result, everyone has been forced to experience a life from within Lucifer's energy mind prison. Every soul has been trapped in a lifelong solitary confinement which is controlled by Lucifer.

Through EGO Lucifer has kept mankind in his energetic mind prison of limitation. It began consciousness man's great energetic oppression. With the energetic blinders of Lucifer turned on for over 6000 years consciousness man has become satisfied, content and complacent in their energetic mind prisons where today they have become the most docile they have ever been. At first glimpse to the mind everything appears to be in perfect order only because the mind is aware of so little.

For 6000 years Lucifer's EGO has completely blinded all of consciousness man to Higher Consciousness. Lucifer has brilliantly denied the existence of a Higher Consciousness so he can be coroneted as Higher Consciousness. He has intentionally sabotaged the energy pregnancy and believes he is now on the cusp of victory.

Through EGO, Lucifer created the traits of man that complement his energy of fear and negativity. Since Adam and Eve he has unleashed traits of doubt, insecurity, hatred, impatience, selfishness and greed and made them consciousness man's foremost traits. These are the weapons he uses to achieve his victory. They are led by doubt, which creates ridicule and scoffing that further spread the seeds of Lucifer's energy.

In order for Lucifer's plans to be fulfilled, EGO must continue to ignite the hatred of man until they annihilate themselves. It could not be any easier; through EGO Lucifer can easily incite man's hatred and bring about his victory.

By controlling the minds of consciousness man it also satisfies Lucifer's massive insecurities. EGO creates his high and makes sure it doesn't stop. For 6000 years whenever he began to come down from his high he would simply explore the world and select his next victim to create his next high. EGO easily satisfies his massive cravings by inciting a level of hatred within a person that manifests itself physically through them in a way that moves him one step closer to securing victory.

Lucifer knows his energy of fear and negativity renders man useless. He knows it will nullify man's mind and only allow it to see what he wishes it to see. His gift to man is doubt and insecurity. It is his child's play. EGO is Lucifer's creation - provided free of charge - so his dreams can come true. It's perfect because no mind will ever want to know about a

Higher Consciousness. Could it be any more perfect than this? The ignorance of consciousness man secures his victory.

EGO keeps man adrift in ignorant darkness within Lucifer's energetic mind prisons. It is how the world must stay for just a little while longer so his destiny can be achieved. Lucifer will always be eternally grateful to you for helping him attain his goal. He is the master of chaos who has waited a long time for Higher Consciousness' energy pregnancy to end. Lucifer's rational for EGO is to provide you with the structure and direction you need, for without it you would not be able to receive his pampering.

EGO has created your fugitive like existence from Higher Consciousness. You are constantly on the run from him, without any idea you are even running away. Does he care? Absolutely not. To him you are nothing more than the means to justify his end.

For Lucifer what began in energetic misery will end in energetic glory. The true master will be exulted. This has been his destiny and since cracking the energy pregnancies source code 6000 years ago he has walked through unscathed. His infinite nightmare is close to ending. "Edging God Out" is the essence of everything that Lucifer does. It is what he has been doing for 6000 years.

Since Adam and Eve, Lucifer has been consciousness man's main power source of fear and negativity. He has produced death to the flesh of man as a result of EGO. This was not Higher Consciousness' intent for consciousness man during its seventh master force.

EGO has made 75 per cent of today's suicides happen because the person has no friends and no hope, which is exactly his goal.

EGO is Lucifer's "dream police correction officers" as it keeps consciousness man trapped and limited in his energetic mind prison. He has temporarily usurped Higher Consciousness' power so his intent can be completed. Through EGO, Lucifer can easily make every accusation against him appear to be heresy. He can deflect any willful separation that denies his goal from being completed. The reality of all accusations against Lucifer's is that they have a zero chance of succeeding because of Lucifer's EGO dream police state that exists everywhere in the world today.

Through EGO, Lucifer is driving the final nail into Higher Consciousness' coffin every second of every day through every action of everyone. EGO is Higher Consciousness' energy tombstone. It denies the mind the opportunity of knowing a Higher Consciousness exists. EGO has atrophied the minds of man by numbing them down into an energetic mush like state.

EGO penetrates into the deepest regions of man's consciousness. The fear that Lucifer has created - to protect what is "ours" - is constantly turned on within all of us on a second-by-second basis. The younger the soul, the greater his triumphs are because he can reveal more to them. EGO places the mind in a constant defense mode within his energetic mind prisons. It helps him achieve his goal by destroying, distracting and limiting our mind through trying to protect "possessions" that EGO uses to satisfy our insecurities. To Lucifer our misery is his delight.

Lucifer uses anything possible to deny Higher Consciousness from entering a mind. As we near December 21, 2082 Lucifer will amp up his control through the law and courts in countries around the world to increase wars, rebellions and atrocities against all of consciousness man. His latest victory is the holy wars of the world that pit religious beliefs against religious beliefs. EGO has also divided sects of similar religious beliefs against each other. EGO has made his victory so easy.

One thing EGO cannot do is sense when Higher Consciousness touches a person's heart and soul. EGO does not have the ability to hack into Higher Consciousness' frequencies of communication. EGO is not on the same channel as your heart and soul's frequencies. Its energetic perfection and perfect love communications cannot be detected by Lucifer or EGO. EGO is powerless to these frequencies.

For 6000 years, EGO has been Lucifer's master deception and derailment to Higher Consciousness' energy pregnancy. If there was no EGO, Higher Consciousness would have easily incarnated itself into every mind. EGO self-programs every mind by understanding, accessing and implementing all required deceptions through its highest vulnerabilities. Each mind is different and Lucifer's EGO knows exactly what winning strings to pull in every mind to prey on its vulnerabilities.

Today's education system is another pillar of "Luciferin" limitation. Here Lucifer can easily address a mind's biggest vulnerability by exciting them with lofty heights of specific knowledge that lead them to take great pride in their accomplishments and superior knowledge so much so they believe they are the Higher Consciousness. Any reference to these poor souls not being "the everything" spews out great animosity and hatred from them.

EGO leads man to believe their highest accountability is to themselves and this is all that matters. For 3.2 million years Lucifer built his EGO through studying the minds of survivalist man. Lucifer has programmed EGO to address every possible aspect that any mind is capable of bringing forward on its own.

Lucifer speeds up the mind through his sludge of knowledge. EGO limits wisdom by filing the mind up for the most part with useless trivia that always limits one's potential. Lucifer uses knowledge to wind us up and keep us on our energetic treadmills: doing the same thing over and over again and expecting different results.

Up until Higher Consciousness' energy pregnancy secret and deification process thoughts are unveiled Lucifer's cloak of darkness will be impossible for you to tear off. It has deformed and limited you because of Lucifer's sizeable entitlement issues.

Lucifer's EGO, which is your great moral paralyzer, has denied you from becoming Higher Consciousness. EGO denies all wisdom and only allows Lucifer's limiting base of knowledge. EGO forces your consciousness to focus only on the outward, not the inward.

Lucifer selfishly split from Higher Consciousness' energy pregnancy intent to forge his own identity. For

6000 years he has led consciousness man along his entitlement pathway.

It is Lucifer that made Higher Consciousness invisible to every mind of consciousness man. Lucifer knows that Higher Consciousness' mercy, compassion and tenderness (contained within its energetic perfection and perfect love) has no answer to overcome his deception.

Lucifer has done everything he can to consciousness man to keep them trapped in his energetic mind prison. To every soul every life experience is a living hell.

Higher Consciousness warned Adam and Eve of Lucifer's plan before Lucifer even hatched it. His warning was to ensure that his final micro- seconds would be completed as it was intended to be.

The minds of consciousness man have been limited by Lucifer for 6000 years. No one has ever wanted their freedom stolen; however, we all have and don't even know it. Higher Consciousness' seventh master force's intent has always meant to reveal its wisdoms of energetic perfection, perfect love and hope to every mind so they could choose to either become Higher Consciousness or deny Higher Consciousness. However, through EGO, Lucifer has cleverly made that decision for us.

Lucifer has successfully turned away the minds of consciousness man from Higher Consciousness to themselves. He has made them believe they are the Higher Consciousness and pain, suffering and lies are the norm.

Because Lucifer has entered the minds of

consciousness man, Higher Consciousness has been forced to cut short the live expectancy of mankind as a means to limit Lucifer.

The sad truth is that consciousness man has devolved to accept their energetic bottom feeder complacency. Lucifer has easily satisfied his entitlement issues by limiting the potential and power of consciousness man. Lucifer's EGO has breached Higher Consciousness and trumped consciousness man by holding them hostage. To the mind, he has literally blotted out Higher Consciousness' from consciousness man.

Lucifer's deception through EGO will profess anything to satisfy your vulnerabilities and satisfy your highest level of insecurity. He will contest every inch of ground if you should ever advance toward Higher Consciousness.

To ensure victory, Lucifer must keep Higher Consciousness' energy pregnancy secret and deification process thoughts from ever seeing the light of day. When it does, he must excite popular indignation against it so it never gains momentum. Until Lucifer takes the reins of Higher Consciousness' Divine Child EGO must continue to keep the pedal to the metal and bring about insincere, regenerative elements of doubt and unbelief that will continue to numb the minds of man.

Lucifer's energetic mind prison is desolate, worthless and barren. From here EGO can easily produce a mind's satisfaction through money that temporally satisfies a person's EGO insecurities. This is Lucifer's carrot he dangles in front of everyone. It is a brilliant scheme because money allows everyone to satisfy his or her insecurities EGO creates. Money is Lucifer's self-fulfilling prophecy that he believes all but guarantees him victory. Round and round the mind goes and where it stops only Lucifer knows.

To ensure victory, EGO has plays on the minds two powerful authorities of reason and logic. Through EGO, if the mind disregards reason and logic he threatens it by withdrawing his drug of money. Money is Lucifer's vice over everyone.

EGO has moved consciousness man to an energetic comatose state whereby everyone is easily controlled and manipulated by Lucifer's drug of money.

Energetically, Lucifer is their god through money. Money is his matrix over life. He believes that through everyone's addiction to money he is infallible.

CHAPTER 23

LUCIFER'S MATRIX

"Reality is merely an illusion, albeit a very persistent one."
Albert Einstein (1879 – 1955)

LUCIFER'S MATRIX PRODUCES life's great drama that happens every second, everywhere for everyone.

It does not matter where you are at in life; energetically you are exactly where you are supposed to be. You have been limited in your life by Lucifer to be exactly where you presently find yourself. Why? So through his money matrix, victory can be achieved. Everyone's soul entered this life experience knowing Lucifer would limit your vessel to the circumstances and life you presently have. To every final life experience soul life is an alternative reality.

For many, your world is mundane. For most it is a place devoid of passion. Around you are the constant reminders of Lucifer's matrix and your consciousness limitations. No one has been allowed to understand their infinite potentials. Everyone's mind is a restrained beacon of hope that has never been allowed to shine.

Lucifer's energy matrix has been designed to limit. Your mind's energy realities are the result of 6000 years of EGO based directives that has brought you to Lucifer's utmost point of compliance, convenience and conformity: meant to keep you and all of mankind in an energetic comatose state.

Morpheus (a fictional character in The Matrix franchise) referred to Lucifer's matrix in the movie this way, "It is everywhere; it is all around us. Even now, in this very room, you can see it when you look out your window, or turn on your television set. You can feel it when you go to work, when you go to church, when you pay taxes. It is the world that has been pulled over your eyes to blind you from the truth."

Lucifer uses his drug of money through a sliding wealth and power matrix. It is very simple and works like this: the more his drug of money controls a mind the easier it is for him to keep you in his energetic mind prison.

The key individuals within Lucifer's wealth and power matrix are his "enlightened ones." They are his energy matrix insiders. The Latin word for Lucifer's energy matrix insiders is *illuminatus* or *illuminati*. It should not be surprising that Lucifer's enlightened ones occupy the top rungs of his wealth and power matrix. Their official title is "investment banker." They are Lucifer's fraternity who control the world's monetary markets. For their role they have been authorized by Lucifer to receive a larger portion of his drug of money.

Not surprisingly, Lucifer has filled his top two rungs

of his wealth and power matrix with families from Higher Consciousness' spiritual first nation. They have been waiting the longest for Higher Consciousness to appear and Lucifer again in his brilliance made them his drug of money gatekeepers and dispensers. They are his investment bankers and most loyal servants. They are Lucifer's drug of money handlers that keep Lucifer's wealth and power matrix churning.

By the 1700s they controlled Europe and then easily infiltrated the fledgling American Government. Today they control the masses of consciousness man for Lucifer through his wealth and power rungs of commerce, government and banking. Lucifer uses these rungs to advance his limitations against consciousness man. For doing so they receive Lucifer's constant wealth and power.

Lucifer is so sure of his wealth and power matrix's success he flaunts it for all to see on the back of the American currency. It has been referred to as his all-seeing eye.

Lucifer's all-seeing eye on the back of the US $1 bill.

Lucifer believes his wealth and power matrix will never be known and has displayed it in plain view for all to see. Lucifer knows that the bottom rung of his wealth and power matrix (which is where 99.9 per cent of mankind reside) are so comatose in his energetic mind prisons that they will never understand his game.

Energetically, Lucifer's capstone is our mind and his all-seeing eye is his EGO. Practically Lucifer controls EGO through money and EGO produces the actions desired by Lucifer who gleefully watches it all.

Lucifer has further deceived the minds of mankind through EGO making the minds of consciousness man believe that money's all-seeing eye represents the eye of God watching over mankind. By providing our minds with his fix to our doubt and insecurity created by EGO, Lucifer is easily able to keep us trapped in his energetic mind prisons to perpetuate his wealth and power matrix.

Everything in the world today (including our minds through EGO) Lucifer controls through money.

Today, we cling to our excess debris like never before. We have become a civilization of hoarders because of our addiction to excess. In 1960, North America had no storage facilities. Today, in North America alone it is estimated there is over 30 billion cubic feet of storage space. The space is leased out to hold the excesses of our debris that our minds cannot consciously rid itself of, even though most of us no longer use or need it. Today the self-storage industry earns in excess of $25 USD billion to store for the most part useless rubble we will never use again.

Lucifer knows he can easily keep our minds trapped in his energetic mind prison because of our minds' need of excess. Excess is our short-term crutch that temporarily eliminates our mind's doubt and insecurity to satisfy EGO. Lucifer has created, through EGO, numerous doubt and insecurity limitations to keep us trapped in his energetic mind prison.

Lucifer's limitations always create stress. The more fearful and insecure we are, the more stressed we become. The more stressed we become the more destructive we are and the greater toll it takes on our mental, emotional, physical and spiritual wellbeing. Our minds have been conditioned to believe that our short-term fix of money satisfies everything.

Lucifer's drug of money is our social contract that temporarily soothes our mind's doubt and insecurity by satisfying EGO. EGO constantly bombards our mind with something that will satisfy its short-term needs. Our energetic reality is the more we have, the more we crave and the more we don't have, the more we want. Our minds are absolutely addicted to money and like any junkie - our mind requires more of it to satisfy its ongoing addiction. Money is Lucifer's drug, which keeps his matrix alive and keeps our minds energetically trapped in his energetic mind prisons.

Lucifer has been able to keep us addicted to his drug money because EGO makes it our minds' energetic fix.

THE HISTORY OF MONEY

Before money, people bartered. The system of barter was an exchange of goods or services for other goods or services; for example, a bag of rice for a bag of beans. However, carrying bags of rice, beans or other commodities became difficult as they would become perishable and difficult to store.

THE BARTER SYSTEM

In 700 BC coins began to appear in the Western world as an exchange to buy and sell. Some of the earliest known paper money dates back to China, where its issuance became common around the year AD 960.

Approximately 350 years ago Lucifer began to create his wealth and power matrix with money. He placed his assets in financial instruments and circulated them through the world as stocks, bonds and debt, which made it impossible to find out the truth regarding Lucifer's energetic essence behind money.

Lucifer creates and controls his social contract of money wherever and whenever he wants. He has made all of us addicts to his drug of money and justifies its existence as doing us a favor.

He has made our reality appear pleasant and acceptable and even justifies his enabling of us. His justification for money is that it makes us feel good. He has made money his matrix to everything. His wealth and power matrix is both feared and loved at the same time.

Money is loved because it produces the roof over our heads and sustenance to survive. Money is feared because of the stress and destruction it creates. Money is what drives the world's economies and builds our consciousness' self-worth. A lack of it produces doubt and insecurity which creates stress. Up until now Lucifer's wealth and power matrix has been hidden from our minds.

Understanding Lucifer's wealth and power matrix is something he doesn't want your mind to know because it begins to unravel EGO and unlock the door of your energetic mind prison. The unlocking of your energetic mind prison door begins with the realization that money is only a commodity, an item of trade or commerce.

Every commodity has a manufacturing and distribution cycle which operates in the following manner:

First, the commodity is produced by the manufacturer. Next, the manufacturer sells their finished commodity to their manufacturing representative for a profit. The manufacturing representative is responsible for distributing the commodity within a large geographical region, such as a country. To effectively distribute the manufactured commodity within its geographical region, the manufacturing representative resells it to a retailer for a profit. The retailer makes the final sale of the commodity to the consumer, for yet another profit.

Lumber is an example of a commodity. The manufacturing and distribution cycle of lumber is as follows:

Step #1 – Trees are cut down and manufactured by a lumber manufacturer in order to produce the finished commodity of lumber.

Step #2 – The lumber manufacturer sells his finished product to his manufacturing rep to distribute it within a large geographical region.

Step #3 – The manufacturing representative resells the lumber to his retailers in smaller geographical areas to sell locally.

Step #4 – The retailer completes the final sale of lumber to the consumer.

What Lucifer has kept hidden from us is that money also follows the same manufacturing and distribution cycle as lumber and every other commodity. However, with money, Lucifer has added extra controls (to his commodity of money), which other commodities do not have. It is through revealing this information that the mind can begin to free itself from Lucifer's energetic mind prison as his energetic matrix of money begins to unravel in your mind.

The manufacturing and distribution cycle of money is as follows:

Step #1 – Money is manufactured by its manufacturer. The manufacturing of money is completed by central banks. The Bank of International Settlements in Basel, Switzerland is the central bank of central banks. It controls all other central banks. Central banks are banking cartels with monolithic powers that create a nation's money supply. The United States' central bank is the Federal Reserve. This gigantic infrastructure and system of commerce is Lucifer's masterpiece. It's his monument that he believes will keep Higher Consciousness away.

"The Federal Reserve is an independent agency and there is no other agency of government which can overrule any actions that we take."
—*Allan Greenspan (b. 1926)*

Unlike lumber and every other manufactured commodity, there are no hard costs to the manufacturing of money. Money manufacturers do

not need to cut down trees like lumber manufacturers. They do not need to extract precious metals from the ground like a precious metal manufacturer does. Money is manufactured out of thin air with only a nominal printing cost associated with it.

Step #2 – Lucifer creates money from thin air through central banks. Unlike other commodities, which sell their commodity to their manufacturing reps for a profit, Lucifer, through his central banks, has no costs and everything he does with money is pure profit and they have no accountability to anyone. To maximize his profit he lends his commodity of money to his manufacturing reps and federal governments in the countries where he prints it. By lending his commodity of money to federal governments, Lucifer still maintains ownership and everything that it has created is the central banks collateral until it is paid back in full. Experts have calculated the world's global net worth to be negative USD$57 trillion based on total global assets estimated of USD$223 trillion and an estimated total global debt of USD$280 trillion.

Federal governments distribute Lucifer's borrowed money within the jurisdiction in which money is printed. There are central banks located in the following countries: Afghanistan, Albania, Algeria, Angola, Argentina, Armenia, Aruba, Australia, Austria, Azerbaijan, Bahamas, Bahrain, Bangladesh, Barbados, Belarus, Belgium, Belize, Benin, Bermuda, Bhutan, Bolivia, Bosnia and Herzegovina, Botswana, Brazil, Burkina Faso, Burundi, Cambodia, Cameroon, Canada, Cape Verde, Cayman Islands, Central African Republic, Chad, Chile, China, Colombia, Congo, The Democratic Republic of the Congo, Costa Rica, Croatia, Cuba, Curaçao, Cyprus, Czech Republic, Denmark, Dominican Republic, Ecuador, Egypt, El Salvador, Equatorial Guinea, Estonia, Ethiopia, European Union, Fiji, Finland, France, Gabon, Gambia, Georgia, Germany, Greece, Guatemala, Guinea, Guinea-Bissau, Guyana, Haiti, Honduras, Hong Kong, Hungary, Iceland, India, Indonesia, Iran, Iraq, Ireland, Israel, Italy, Jamaica, Japan, Jordan, Kazakhstan. Kenya, Korea, Kosovo, Kuwait, Kyrgyzstan, Lao, Latvia, Lebanon, Lesotho, Liberia, Libya, Lithuania, Luxembourg, Macao, Macedonia, MadagaHCAr, Malawi, Malaysia, Mali, Malta, Mauritius, Mexico, Moldova, Mongolia, Montenegro, Morocco, Mozambique, Myanmar, Namibia, Nepal, Netherlands, New Zealand, Nicaragua, Niger, Nigeria, Norway, Oman, Organization of Eastern Caribbean States, Pakistan, Papua New Guinea, Paraguay, Peru, Philippines, Poland, Portugal, Qatar, Romania, Russian Federation, Rwanda, Samoa, San Marino, Saudi Arabia, Senegal, Serbia, Seychelles, Sierra Leone,

Singapore, Slovakia, Slovenia, Solomon Islands, South Africa, Spain, Sri Lanka, Sudan, Suriname, Swaziland, Sweden, Switzerland, Syrian Arab Republic, Tajikistan, Tanzania, Thailand, Togo, Tonga, Trinidad and Tobago, Tunisia, Turkey, Turkmenistan, Uganda, Ukraine, United Arab Emirates, United Kingdom, United States, Uruguay, Uzbekistan, Vanuatu, Venezuela, Vietnam, Yemen, Zambia and Zimbabwe.

Borrowing means to receive something temporarily from its owner who's expects it back with interest. Money is borrowed by governments of the world who are in huge debt to the central bankers who have lent it to them. A government's collateral (to the central bankers for their debt) is the assets within their country. Therefore, because of government debt the assets we think are ours - are not. Behind the scenes, secretly, for the right to borrow money governments have pledged as collateral to the central bankers all of their nations wealth. Lucifer has lulled us into a false sense of security that we own whatever his borrowed drug of money has produced. Even though it may be in your bank account or it may be in assets you own, the real owner of it is your countries central bank and always will be until your countries debt is paid back to the central bankers.

In Lucifer's matrix, our mind has been tricked to believe that we own money. However, it's not ours, it never was and it never will be. This was evidenced in March 2013 in Cyprus where the biggest bank heist of all time occurred. Bank depositors – Cypriots - had six billion Euros stolen from their bank accounts overnight to pay back money owed to the central bankers. This led Jeroen Dijsselbloem, at the time, the Dutch head of Eurozone finance ministers, to boast this would be the model for future bailouts. Beware: Lucifer has put the plans in motion so that one night very soon he will strike the massive blow against all of consciousness man's assets just like his dry run did in Cyprus.

Lucifer, through his central bankers, has revealed his plans of how to take back money that we think is ours and the Cyprus heist shows how easy it is for him to do. The Cyprus heist was Lucifer's dry run to gauge what kind of reaction there would be when money vanishes. Cyprus is only the beginning.

We are all merely money junkies who have been taught to hoard our fix and do everything possible to make sure we never run out of it.

From his position of power and as the owner of money, Lucifer has always been calling the shots in his matrix. He controls all governments by financing them. He has perfected his control over all governments, as governments require money in order to survive. Lucifer always has his wealth and power top rungs hiding behind the scenes as they pull the strings for everything he wants his matrix to do. He controls the media, the governments, the central intelligence agencies, the banks, the stock markets and virtually every other aspect in his horizontal, linear, measured matrix. This has allowed him to easily control the minds of consciousness man because of our addiction to money.

"Some of the biggest men in the United States are afraid of something. They know there is a power

somewhere, so organized, so subtle, so watchful, so interlocked, so complete, so pervasive that they had better not speak above their breath when they speak in condemnation of it."
—President Woodrow Wilson (1856-1924)

Step #3 – Lending money to governments is how Lucifer holds absolute power over all nations and mankind. Lucifer knows he is insulated and safe because governments control the people in their country through law enforcement agencies and ultimately the military if the people become restless.

Lucifer's main commerce game is capitalism. The business of the capitalist in Lucifer's matrix is the management of capital. Governments lend Lucifer's borrowed money to their retailers, who are the banks and brokerage houses within the geographical jurisdiction that money is printed in.

"Who controls the money can control the world."
—Henry Kissinger (b.1923)

"It is well enough that people of the nation do not understand our banking and monetary system, for if they did, I believe there would be a revolution before tomorrow morning."
—Henry Ford (1863–1947)

The insiders of capitalism are mobile; they do not get tied to any given location. Capital is very fluid and liquid. It flows to where growth is realized the fastest. We see this today with the countless number of ghost towns that exist globally.

Another popular game played by Lucifer creates profits through war. Lucifer finances both sides of military conflicts. This can be seen over the last 100 years beginning with World War I.

Recently, Lucifer ratcheted war up to its highest stakes by pitting faiths and religions against each other. Holy wars, wars of religions and faith are Lucifer's ultimate type of war because now man's spiritual emotion of faith has been brought into the equation of war. These types of wars will never end. This is exactly what Lucifer wants. To Lucifer, war is his casino and the gamblers in his casino battle long and hard to borrow more chips of money from him to finance the war. Lucifer downloads his will to his top aides who carry out his intent of who will be the victor and the last man standing in all wars.

Wars are always the most profitable game of Lucifer's matrix because he also gets to manage the aftermath and reconstruction whenever wars end. In wars millions of people die and while the world mourns, Lucifer already has his post-war reconstruction investments in place to maximize his profits.

It became inevitable that the law of diminishing returns would someday overthrow capitalism. The decline of capitalism began around 1970. This was when capitalism was forced to create greater returns in another way because of relatively flat production levels and consumption. Capitalism began to move production to low income areas of the world in order to produce greater profit margins. As a result, capitalism has had four decades of artificial growth.

The end of capitalism was in September of 2008, with the financial collapse that brought the global financial system to its knees and vaporized in excess of five trillion dollars just from the US economy.

Lucifer thinks and plans how his matrix will be rolled out many decades in advance and downloads its plans to his top investment bankers who begin to plan accordingly. To Lucifer, his matrix is like a game of chess and he owns and controls all the pieces on the chessboard, including the minds of humanity. He decides how much money to print and he only prints as much as he needs in order to use it as he sees fit to bring about his end goal. Lucifer is our real-life Monopoly banker.

Capitalism was handy, but it ran its course in 2008, as he planned. Lucifer officially brought capitalism to its knees in 2008, but this plan was revealed to his wealth and power matrix top rungs decades before it actually happened. It blew apart based on a controlled demolition of real estate bubbles and toxic derivatives. Since 2008 Lucifer has also withdrawn cash from his matrix to the point now where it is entirely run on debt created by keystrokes. This has set him up for his next great heist which will steal back all of the world's assets to pay back the central bankers debt. The central bankers call for governments to payback their debt has begun in all countries throughout the world and as each day passes we are one day closer to becoming the paupers Lucifer has planned us to be.

Like any great creator, Lucifer creates from the back end knowing what he wants to accomplish, and then fills in the details in order to make it work. Post capitalism was created this same way. Post capitalism can be traced back to 1980 in the US and the UK. In Europe the Maastricht Treaty (signed on February 7, 1992) led to the creation of the Euro. The new game began to reveal itself with privatization, free trade agreements and the establishment of the regulation busting World Trade Organization, as Lucifer prepared his New World Order and next game of globalization.

Since 2008 globalization has accelerated rapidly. The new regime of global government is being established in order to replace the existing forms of government. This can be seen with the creation of the World Trade Organization, the International Monetary Fund and the World Bank. Globalization. Lucifer's new world order has already begun to carve the world into super states. The European Union and African Union are already a reality, while the North American Union of Canada, the United States and Mexico will soon become a reality along with Asia's Pacific Union.

Globalization has already started within the corporate world. In the United States the number of corporations controlling the US media has amalgamated from 50 to 5 since 1983. Get ready for the marching orders of globalization as they come directly from Lucifer through his central bank of central banks.

The game of globalization will be for Lucifer's wealth and power matrix's top rung to control. There will be fewer moving parts in Lucifer's matrix to manage. Instead of dealing with all of the various countries' governments, it will become centralized and easier to run. As we speak Lucifer is restructuring and downsizing his machine in order to maximize profits. He is currently preparing to downsize his machine by shedding himself of the expense created by countless governments. Globalization is Lucifer's downsizing and restructuring of his world corporation. It would appear to be a brilliant scheme, if your part of Lucifer's top rung in his wealth and power matrix. However only about .000002 per cent of mankind is part of this rung.

Lucifer began globalization slowly. Over the last 40 years he tried it out by introducing policies and practices in Third World countries where the resistance would be minimal. However, he has now begun to transition these policies to First World countries. As in all Third World countries, mass poverty and police state tyranny is right around the corner for those living in First World countries.

The anti-globalist movement began resisting globalization. It started near the end of the twentieth century as more and more people began to understand what globalization really meant. This concerned Lucifer. How dare his slaves blindly not accept what he is doing as they have always done in the past.

In November of 1999, Lucifer tipped his hand by

authorizing a police state tyranny response against the resistance to globalization in Seattle, Washington. This included incapacitating people by holding their eyes open and pepper spraying them. The Seattle police response actually helped strengthen the anti-globalization movement, globally more and more people began to see Lucifer's next game and didn't like it. This peaked in July 2001, in Genoa, Italy, when violence from both sides resembled a war.

Lucifer knew consciousness man's growing resistance to globalization had to stop because it was getting to close to revealing his intent. This change became a reality on September 11, 2001. On this fateful day globalization went underground and disappeared from our public consciousness. In an instant, Lucifer had successfully deflected our attention away from globalization, toward a whole new enemy. New wars were started as Lucifer began his most profitable game of war all over again.

Globalization ushers in Lucifer's new game in his post- capitalism era. The one-world system is fast approaching. Lucifer has created his new global culture and control mechanisms of poverty and regimentation. It controls those who live in First World countries similar to what has happened to those who live in Third World countries. The only thing standing in the way of the successful implementation of Lucifer's end game is the incarnation of Higher Consciousness into consciousness man that has been successfully denied by Lucifer for 6000 years. This has never been more needed than it is today as Higher Consciousness'

December 21, 2082 Divine Child's energy birth approaches.

Step #4 – Money retailers make their final sale of money to consumers, adding yet another premium to it. Banks sell money to the public at prime +. Initially, less risky ventures were charged a lower interest rate, while riskier ventures were charged a higher interest rate. Lucifer has even allowed banks to create their own mini credit matrix by the issuance of credit to consumers. By giving us a false sense of security through credit, Lucifer can easily has keep our minds from knowing his true intentions and the larger plans he has in store for us.

With the exception of money, this is where a commodity's manufacturing and distribution cycle ends – not so for Lucifer. He has added two additional control mechanisms against us to get back as much of his manufactured commodity of money as possible.

To satisfy his massive insecurities and fear regarding his matrix being exposed; he needed to place more

control over us. He has done so with two added monetary control mechanisms.

Luciferian Control Mechanism #1 is about taking back from us as much of his manufactured commodity of money as possible. This control mechanism is similar to a computer manufacturer legally stealing back one-half of a computer we just bought from him.

This is what Lucifer does with money. He accomplishes this with taxes, fees and levies through his wholesale distributor of governments. Taxes will never stop being levied; they will only continue to increase with more new taxes, fees and levies being instituted to take away as much money from us as possible. This is an absolute guarantee.

In many countries around the world taxes were introduced as a temporary means to fund World War I. Here is a partial list of some of today's taxes and fees levied by governments: accounts receivable tax, airline surcharge tax, airline fuel tax, airport maintenance tax, building permit tax, cigarette tax, corporate income tax, death tax, dog license tax, driving permit tax, environmental tax, excise tax, federal income tax, federal unemployment tax, fishing license tax, food license tax, gasoline tax, goods and services tax, gross receipts tax, harmonized sales tax, hunting license tax, hydro tax, inheritance tax, interest tax, liquor tax, luxury taxes, marriage license tax, Medicare tax, mortgage tax, personal income tax, property tax, prescription drug tax, provincial income tax, provincial sales tax, real estate tax, recreational vehicle tax, retail sales tax, service charge tax, school tax, federal, provincial and municipal telephone surcharge taxes, telephone minimum usage surcharge tax, vehicle license registration tax, vehicle sales tax, water tax, watercraft registration tax, well permit tax and workers compensation tax.

I am sure there are more government taxes, fees and levies I have missed, but you get the picture. Lucifer has made sure a tax structure is enforced in most countries in order to take back from us as much of his manufactured commodity of money as possible. This satisfies his massive fears and insecurities and keeps us from exposing his game. It also keeps our minds locked away in his energetic mind prison, addicted and needing the next fix of his money.

Luciferin Control Mechanism #2 is again about legally stealing back as much of his social contract of money as possible. This is similar to a computer manufacturer charging us a user fee to store our half a computer within his storage facility. This is what banks do with money. They charge us transaction fees on everything we do in their bank for the privilege of keeping our after-tax money with them.

In the first quarter of 2010, the total profits of Canada's six biggest banks surged to $5.3 billion dollars. The first quarter profit of the Bank of Nova Scotia was $988 million; the Canadian Imperial Bank of Commerce was $652 million; the Bank of Montreal was $657 million; National Bank was $215 million; the Royal Bank was $1.5 billion; and TD Canada Trust was $1.29 billion. Ironically, some of this profit was a result of the fees banks charged us for the privilege of holding our money.

"The obsession for maximizing profits to shareholders has got to be seen as abusive, as dangerous and as one of the most appalling situations on this planet because it makes for criminal behavior."
—Anita Roddick, Founder of The Body Shop (b.1942)

Through EGO Lucifer always makes us feel unworthy without his drug of money. And Lucifer makes sure every generation proves the past

generation's breakthroughs are fleeting based on newer more exciting technologies. However, presently Lucifer has our energetic treadmills moving so fast that present-day technologies become obsolete many times before they are ever revealed to the public.

The underlying principle of today's Luciferian education is curriculum control that enslaves us and moves us in his chosen directional limitations. Obviously this helps Lucifer achieve his end goal much easier because it enhances our addiction to money.

Lucifer has made us "money drunk" like never before, with wealth and possessions to secure victory. He knows that through EGO, our minds will never choose against his drug of money that satisfies all of our insecurities. He knows he has presented the world (to the minds of consciousness man) in his best light so that they choose his drug of money. He has protected his essence of money so it can never be used against him. He knows if he were to start losing control of his drug of money, his matrix would crumble. This is why he has taken all the necessary precautions to make sure this never happens. EGO has created a form for man to crave pleasure and lust that strikes at the very core of our emotional existence. Thus, Lucifer believes, no man can ever deny him.

Religion started off with the absolute best intentions of helping us move closer to Higher Consciousness. At its infancy it was something Lucifer did not know how to control. However, Lucifer figured out that religion is also very easy to control, just like consciousness man it can be done through money. Sadly, today mainstream religion is nothing more than Lucifer's stonewalling pulpit that has failed to move a single person any closer to understanding Higher Consciousness' true intent.

For centuries Lucifer has hijacked religion; who selfishly endeavored to satisfy their insecurities by robbing the poor to grow their coffers. Through EGO Lucifer has denied the original true intent of religion by building colossal shrines and temples. These can be seen around the world as the hierarchy of every religion; they've inappropriately used the donations of its members to satisfy their EGO rather than nourish the needs of mankind as they purport to do.

Today, through Lucifer's matrix, he controls us like never before. It does not matter which political party is in control of a country's federal government the outcome will always be what Lucifer dictates. During these final days Lucifer's goal is simple: keep us trapped in his energetic mind prisons through our addiction to his social contract of money.

The Gross World Product (GWP) is the combined gross national product of every country in the world. GWP is the balance between global imports and exports. In 2012 the GWP totaled US$84.97 trillion. This produced a per-person GWP capita of approximately USD$11,800 per person and is what Lucifer creates through his central banks to keep his game alive.

Lucifer has no intent to let our minds out of his energetic mind prison. In fact, the more we are addicted to his drug of money the easier it is for him to keep us locked up in them.

Perhaps it was the 14th Dalai Lama of Tibet (b.1935)

who summed it up best, "He sacrifices his health in order to make money. Then he sacrifices money to replicate his health. And then he is so anxious about the future that he does not enjoy the present; the result being that he does not live in the present or the future; he lives as if he is never going to die, and then dies having never really lived."

PART V: APPLYING THE SECRET

CHAPTER 24

THE APOCALYPSES OF HIGHER CONSCIOUSNESS

THE INTENT OF HIGHER CONSCIOUSNESS' seventh master force, which was unleashed 6000 years ago from its energy matrix, is to complete its energy labor through incarnating into the minds of consciousness man so its Divine Child energy birth can begin on December 21, 2082.

When Higher Consciousness' seventh master force was unleashed everything in its energy fetus was percolating along exactly as intended. Higher Consciousness had placed Adam and Eve in their utopian paradise without any cares or concerns. They were exactly where they were meant to be so Higher Consciousness could incarnate into Adam and Eve. Everything was moving along perfectly until Lucifer's betrayal.

Without Lucifer's betrayal there would have been no hiccups in Higher Consciousness' 13.75 billion year energy blueprint. Its seventh master force would have completed its deification process in all of its 100 trillion energy cells. Every atom of every cell would have subatomically been deified as Higher Consciousness so its Divine Child energy birth would begin as scheduled.

The Divine Child can only be the energetic perfection and perfect love that Higher Consciousness is. Lucifer is not this. Lucifer had been a vital cog for 13.72 billion years in making the energy birth possible through the completion of Higher Consciousness' first four master forces, but he is not the architect. There is no doubt that Lucifer's efforts in completing Higher Consciousness' energy fetus conception and gestation are commendable, but they do not justify his contempt.

Lucifer is purposely denying Higher Consciousness from completing its energy pregnancy. He is purposely denying the unleashing of your Higher Consciousness incarnation of infinite potentials and immortality that would have already happened.

For 6000 years Lucifer's betrayal has forced you to live a life with massive mind limitations. As a result your mind has been stunted by EGO. The result has significantly crippled you from unleashing your infinite potentials, which you already should have unleashed.

When Lucifer betrayed Higher Consciousness in the Garden of Eden: he forced Higher Consciousness to remove all anti-matter from all of its 100 trillion energy cells. No Higher Consciousness energy of energetic perfection and perfect love could no longer comingle with Lucifer's fear and negativity energy.

Higher Consciousness' energetic potential and perfect love is anti-matter. The result of Lucifer's betrayal has left all 100 trillion energy cells of Higher Consciousness' energy fetus completely devoid of antimatter.

During the energy fetus' energy conception and gestation until Lucifer's betrayal, all 100 trillion energy cells included a Higher Consciousness' perfect symmetric balance and even mixture of matter and antimatter. Today, the asymmetry of matter and anti-matter within the Universe remains one of science's greatest unresolved issues. It is an absolute consciousness limitation. The answer as to "why" rests directly with Lucifer's betrayal.

Higher Consciousness could have obliterated Lucifer 6000 years ago with his betrayal but did not. For approximately 2500 years after Lucifer's betrayal, Higher Consciousness watched as Lucifer implanted his EGO into all of consciousness man's left temples. It was at this time that Higher Consciousness implemented its first energetic apocalypse against Lucifer.

While Lucifer was ratcheting up his EGO controls to higher frequencies against consciousness man, Higher Consciousness met with Moses. Their private ten-day summit took place on Mount Sinai. The purpose of this summit was twofold. First to offset Lucifer's EGO within the minds of Higher Consciousness' spiritual first nation and second to reveal Higher Consciousness' physical incarnate potential for consciousness man.

During their summit, Moses authorized Higher Consciousness to incarnate into him. Up until Moses' death, it was Higher Consciousness through Moses that led the people. However, it was at the death of Moses that Higher Consciousness' ultimate gift for consciousness man was revealed: physical ascension. The ascension of Moses' flesh revealed Higher Consciousness' ultimate gift for consciousness man.

For the next 1500 years, Higher Consciousness monitored the effect of its first apocalypse on consciousness man. During this time, Lucifer ratcheted up its intensity through EGO that placed all souls in a deeper slumber.

With time ticking away until the energy birth, Higher Consciousness' patience reached its breaking point. It was evident that Lucifer had no intentions of ever reversing his actions. In order for Higher Consciousness' Divine Child to have any possibility of being born on December 21, 2082, Higher Consciousness had no choice other than to energetically remove the energy toxicity of Lucifer from itself.

Higher Consciousness' second energy apocalypse began when it cut out the energy of Lucifer from its left eye. Lucifer was energetically changing Higher Consciousness' left eye energy from its energetic perfection and perfect love into Lucifer's toxic energy of fear and negativity. It had begun to impair Higher Consciousness' left eye vision and would have eventually destroyed Higher Consciousness if it had not severed Lucifer. Also, if it had not severed Lucifer from its left eye when it did, its Divine Child would have been stillborn on December 21, 2082.

No longer attached to Higher Consciousness, Lucifer

has been dependent on stealing energy from the souls of consciousness man.

Souls are Higher Consciousness' angel energy threads. They are its energetic perfection and perfect love energy Lucifer requires to survive. Lucifer has discovered how to delay a soul from returning to Higher Consciousness in the divine realm after the body it was trapped in dies. He does so by keeping them in his energetic purgatory state between the divine realm and the physical realm. In Lucifer's energetic purgatory state he becomes the soul's energetic vampire. Here he sucks the soul of its Higher Consciousness energy.

Lucifer's largest heist of Higher Consciousness energy happens through the youngest of souls in the physical realm. Lucifer's craftiness persuades them to sell their complete soul to him while living in the physical realm. To these souls he simply grants them monetary wealth. Through the stealing of Higher Consciousness energy he is able to feed himself.

Upon severing Lucifer as its left eye male consciousness Higher Consciousness began to repair its left eye. It created its physical embodiment of what Lucifer was intended to be. Lucifer immediately recognized Higher Consciousness' physical embodiment when it appeared in the physical realm. Seeing this he ordered all boys two years old and younger (within the region where its physical embodiment was born), to be killed. Lucifer knew Jesus was not just another consciousness man with only a soul: but Jesus was the left eye energy and consciousness of Higher Consciousness.

For nearly 30 years Lucifer unsuccessfully tried to install his EGO within the mind of Jesus but could not. Jesus was safely tucked away in Egypt and energetically protected from Lucifer by Higher Consciousness' energy vortex and second sanctuary. Here Jesus was schooled by Higher Consciousness on top of its second sanctuary and learned everything about Higher Consciousness's deification process and energy pregnancy. He learned how consciousness has been limited by Lucifer and EGO. Jesus was totally prepared by Higher Consciousness when his ministry began.

Subatomically every atom of Jesus was the energetic perfection and perfect love of Higher Consciousness. Its energy pregnancy secret and deification process thoughts was made known to Jesus exactly as it had been made known to Lucifer. Higher Consciousness zinged Jesus with its energy that would always protect Jesus against Lucifer. Jesus was Higher Consciousness' male consciousness that could not cave to Lucifer as Adam and Eve did.

After 30 years of preparation, Higher Consciousness' second energetic apocalypse took place when Jesus and Lucifer physically met.

It took place in the wilderness far away from consciousness man. Jesus had fasted for 40 days and 40 nights to strengthen his resolve against his forthcoming encounter with Lucifer.

Lucifer tried three times to defeat Jesus. Each time was an attempt to take away one of Higher Consciousness seventh master force attributes of energetic perfection, perfect love or hope.

Lucifer tried to steal away Higher Consciousness' energetic perfection attribute by asking Jesus to turn stones to bread in order to sustain life. If agreed to by Jesus, it would have stolen Higher Consciousness' deification energetic perfection wellness attribute.

Lucifer next tried to steal away Higher Consciousness' perfect love attribute by asking Jesus to throw himself down. If agreed to by Jesus, it would have stolen Higher Consciousness' deification perfect love wisdom attribute.

Finally, Lucifer tried to steal away Higher Consciousness' hope attribute, which was added into the seventh master force because of Lucifer's betrayal. Lucifer showed Jesus all his riches. If agreed to by Jesus, Lucifer would have stolen Higher Consciousness' deification hope monetary wealth attribute.

This was Higher Consciousness' second energy apocalypse. Higher Consciousness had hoped Jesus would be its final apocalypse and he would defeat Lucifer. But it was not enough as evidenced by today's Luciferian prevailing fear and negativity energy. Lucifer has successfully deflected his encounter with Jesus to not expose his energetic feebleness.

The sabotaging of Higher Consciousness' energy pregnancy must be stopped. It can only be stopped through Higher Consciousness' final energy apocalypse which will defeat Lucifer's EGO.

For 6000 years Higher Consciousness has painfully watched Lucifer speed up the minds of consciousness man to their present day state of dizziness. For all intents and purpose he has removed any and all semblance of a Higher Consciousness from them. Lucifer has estranged consciousness man from Higher Consciousness and made him an alien to them.

Today, in the final microseconds of Higher Consciousness' energy day, its seventh master force must extinguish Lucifer and all of his fear and negativity energy. Higher Consciousness' energy labor cannot begin with any Lucifer fear and negativity energy. It must be extinguished in order for the Divine Child's energy birth to begin. Instead of 6000 years with no Luciferin interference as Higher Consciousness' seventh master force intended, there are only a few years left to complete its seventh master force intent.

Higher Consciousness' seventh master force's intent has always been to incarnate itself into the minds of consciousness man.

With Higher Consciousness there is no force, no games, no pressure, no trouble, no stress, no pain, no duress, no intimidation, no violence and no coercion. The intent of its seventh master force has always been for the minds of consciousness man to choose their fate. Either they will authorize Higher Consciousness to incarnate into them or they won't.

Higher Consciousness never intended to experience any energy apocalypse; however, because of Lucifer's betrayal they had to happen. Higher Consciousness' final energy apocalypse must permanently triumph over Lucifer's forces of evil.

Again, if Lucifer had not betrayed Higher Consciousness, all of consciousness man would have been energetically vibrating with anticipation counting down the seconds to their flesh's physical ascension onto the Divine Child.

Six thousand years ago Lucifer's betrayal forced Higher Consciousness to scatter its consciousness man family and cut short their life expectancies.

It was during this time that Higher Consciousness needed to learn how to remove Lucifer, EGO and all of his energy of fear and negativity from the energy fetus.

Higher Consciousness' final energy apocalypse must extinguish Lucifer and all of its dark force energy of fear and negativity from its energy fetus so the Divine Child's energy birth can begin on December 21, 2082.

Lucifer's EGO energy lie of "When you listen to me I'll provide you with everything you need" must be removed from the minds of all final-life experience souls.

CHAPTER 25

TODAY'S SEVENTH MASTER FORCE

THE INTENT OF HIGHER CONSCIOUSNESS' seventh master force has always been to complete its energy labor by incarnating subatomically into every atom of your mind. However, due to Lucifer's betrayal Higher Consciousness must also again incarnate subatomically into every one of your body's atoms like it did during its sixth master force.

It is only through your authorization that this can happen as did it with Moses and Jesus. With Higher Consciousness' seventh master force deification attainment every one of your atoms strong nuclear force can be ready to unleash your physical ascension on December 21, 2082 onto Higher Consciousness' Divine Child.

Unleashing your infinite potentials has always been Higher Consciousness' seventh master force intent.

Unfortunately due to Lucifer's betrayal you have

been denied 6000 years in your utopian paradise to enjoy your infinite potentials as Higher Consciousness.

Time is now of the essence and Higher Consciousness needs your authorization to incarnate itself into you.

As Lucifer's attempted hijacking of Jesus revealed, Higher Consciousness has needed to add one extra energy attribute into its seventh master force that was not originally there in order to extinguish Lucifer and all of his energy of fear and negativity once and for all from its energy fetus. Its seventh master force's extra energy aspect of hope has been added to void Lucifer's energy behind his drug of money and substitute it with the energy of Higher Consciousness' energetic perfection and perfect love. Higher Consciousness must become the driving energy force of money so it can be used in a completely different way. The energy of Lucifer behind money has you working for it, while Higher Consciousness will work it for you.

Higher Consciousness always designed you to be the best you've ever been through its seventh master force. If this is your soul's final life experience (as many of us are) you are exactly where you are meant to be. In other words you are right now exactly the person you were meant to be 6000 years ago if Lucifer had not exercised his greed and selfishness.

Lucifer has forced every soul to experience many more life experiences than was originally intended for them to have. Your souls extra life experiences have afforded Higher Consciousness the opportunity to study EGO and add its extra hope aspect into its seventh master force to eradicate Lucifer which must include his energy behind money.

Everyone's Higher Consciousness' deification attainment must first begin by changing your energetic disposition from mind-body-soul to soul-body-mind. Ever since the release of Higher Consciousness' seventh master force 6000 years ago, this has always been the pre-requisite of Higher Consciousness' deification process.

During your soul's final between life experience debriefing with Higher Consciousness in the divine realm, your soul was zinged with Higher Consciousness' energy password of "deification process" that can awaken your soul to begin your energetic disposition change. Every final-life experience soul can awaken from its energetic slumber to be re-activated with Higher Consciousness.

"Deification process" is every final-life experience soul's crowing cock and rooster cry that EGO will try and deny.

CHAPTER 26

PENETRATING EGO

"Change is the law of life. And those who look only to the
past are certain to miss the future."
John F. Kennedy (1917–1963)

CONSCIOUSNESS MAN'S ENERGY pregnancy secret
and deification process has always meant to be
unveiled during Higher Consciousness' seventh master
force.

It is your soul's energetic Holy Grail that has built
into every soul long before the beginning of time.

Since Eden souls have been trapped in Lucifer's
energetic mind prison. To the soul life is an alternate
reality of fear, negativity, chaos and pain. It is the souls
living hell. For the last 6000 years science, religion,
philosophy and spirituality have provided the soul with
glimmers of hope that have helped persevere us from
completely eradicating our species. However, Higher
Consciousness' hands have been tied from unleashing
its seventh master force intent because its energy

pregnancy secret and deification process thoughts had not yet been unveiled. It is beyond our present limits of consciousness and cannot be processed within our consciousness limitations.

Applying your souls Higher Consciousness' energy password frees you from Lucifer's energetic mind prison. It will unleash your Higher Consciousness infinite potentials in ways you never thought imaginable.

EGO has made sure that none of Higher Consciousness' wisdom and illumination has ever been made known. Lucifer further knows that in order for Higher Consciousness to be victorious and birth its Divine Child, a battle of epic energetic proportion between Higher Consciousness and itself would have to take place in your mind. This battle will either extinguish EGO or make it stronger.

To ensure his victory, Lucifer has numbed your mind down with the trivialities of knowledge that overwhelm your mind to create mistaken priorities that deflect it away from the existence of Higher Consciousness. Lucifer knows that without your mind knowing that Higher Consciousness exists, it ensures him victory. It will provide him with the energetic summary judgement he requires as he will be the only energy that shows up at the Divine Child's birth.

Lucifer's justification to the Divine Child could then easily could be, "I am your primary force and the proof is I am the only one here."

You are Higher Consciousness' first sanctuary. You are what must ignite its second sanctuary capstone in order to complete the energy fetus' energy labor.

Every final-life experience soul has been energetically encrypted with High Consciousness soul awakening password to penetrate EGO. When your soul awakens Higher Consciousness can crack open Lucifer's impregnable fortress to penetrate into your mind's vast energy vacuum of blackness that Lucifer has controlled.

Without the betrayal of Lucifer, Higher Consciousness would not have needed to add its energy password at your soul's last debriefing. Without EGO, your soul would have already transformed your consciousness energetic disposition from mind-body-soul to your divine consciousness energetic disposition of soul-body-mind thousands of years ago.

Higher Consciousness' requires you to authorize your deification process. This is Lucifer's pet peeve and why EGO has never allowed your mind to know anything about the existence of Higher Consciousness.

Your mind must choose what is best for you. Either you remain caught up in Lucifer's EGO-led choices or you authorize Higher Consciousness to extinguish EGO and unlock your Higher Consciousness infinite potential and bliss.

Through the unleashing of Higher Consciousness' seventh master force, your Higher Consciousness incarnation must occur prior to December 21, 2082.

Six thousand years ago a dark and threatening day appeared through Lucifer's betrayal. Today that dark day has grown to be legally protected through the courts of all countries. Today, every country's Administration of Justice significantly limits consciousness man from infringing upon Lucifer attaining his goal.

Every country's Administration of Justice's primary purpose is to protect its citizens. However, below the surface of their laws is the absolute protection of Lucifer's drug of money. Administration of Justice's everywhere behold themselves to the central bankers who lend governments the money to survive. Administration of Justices are a government's internal control mechanism which ensures that Lucifer's drug of money flow will not be interrupted.

Lucifer has set up every government to regulate and enforce his intent to completion. Lucifer controls every citizen in every country from causing any interruptions to his "money matrix" through their Administration of Justice. There is no requirement in any country that authorizes a central bank to give one iota of information regarding what it does to anyone. This is the central tenet of every country's Administration of Justice.

A country's central bank are its legal gangsters who have carte blanche authority to carry out anything they want without being culpable to anyone. It's absolutely brilliant on the part of Lucifer as every citizen (of every country) lives in fear - based upon their central bank whims. There are no safeguards or protection in any country that can stop a central bank from doing anything it wants to do. To the central bankers (everyone except Lucifer's 144,000 *illuminati* elite), every life is a worthless pawn that only serves to complete Lucifer's goal.

The changing of everyone's energetic disposition must happen to stop Lucifer.

Your soul is of course familiar with Higher Consciousness energy password. It also knows that Higher Consciousness' seventh master force requires at least 144,000 souls to be incarnated by Higher Consciousness prior to December 21, 2082.

Your soul further knows that the deification process is achieved through Higher Consciousness Activations, (HCA) which re-activate your soul, this time in the physical realm with Higher Consciousness.

After your HCA re-activation, Higher Consciousness reinforces itself in your mind through exiting through your minds back entrance. Lucifer does not even know your mind has a back entrance. Higher Consciousness solidifies itself in your mind by incarnating through your collective unconsciousness into your unconsciousness, subconscious and into your consciousness. Once your mind has been incarnated by Higher Consciousness its final energy apocalypse with Lucifer begins.

This is your minds Energetic Armageddon. Upon extinguishing EGO from your mind Higher Consciousness can begin to unleash its three seventh master force attributes that are built into its seventh master force. They are its energetic perfection attribute and your infinite wellness potential; its perfect love attribute and your infinite wisdom potential; and its hope attribute and your infinite monetary wealth potential.

With your incarnated infinite potentials unleashed your life will never be the same as you count down the days and minutes until your physical ascension onto Higher Consciousness' Divine Child.

Your assurance of Higher Consciousness incarnating into your flesh and attaining your mind and bodies immortality is your soul's final evolutionary step. It is why your soul has always existed. So great is your soul's freedom, purpose and evolution that it transported back and forth countless times to receive its next life experience directives so it could ultimately complete its evolution as you.

Your Higher Consciousness deification is engineered through the passion of your soul to complete its evolution. Its evolution can only be completed through your humility and sincerity; it will never force you to do anything that you do not feel is right. If your mind's light of Higher Consciousness is not strong enough at this time for you to complete your HCA's, know that the light Higher Consciousness has placed in your mind can never go out no matter how hard Lucifer tries to do so. It will always be Lucifer's Achilles heel in your mind as he watches your ember of Higher Consciousness flicker.

Some minds may be overwhelmed with excitement as Higher Consciousness enters. If this is you, it will provide the gratitude and joy your mind has been lacking. It may produce questions that need to be answered before the next stage of your deification process can proceed. Welcome it!

Your soul knows when Higher Consciousness enters your mind it has invaded Lucifer's turf and its powers of darkness will be aroused to great vigilance against it. Every effort of Higher Consciousness advancing itself within your mind will be duly noted by Lucifer. It is his portent of danger. He knows if Higher Consciousness is allowed to shine unobstructed he will lose his foothold in your mind. It will extinguish EGO and allow your mind to become Higher Consciousness.

As Lucifer attempts to keep control of your mind beware as the very existence of your mind holding any Higher Consciousness' light could excite hatred and persecution by Lucifer through others against you.

The awakening of your soul begins your soul's passion and desire to fulfill its freedom, purpose and evolution by deifying your mind and body into Higher Consciousness before December 21, 2082.

Six thousand years of Higher Consciousness' seventh master force signs and wonders are about to be manifested through you in these final micro seconds of Higher Consciousness' day as Higher Consciousness prepares itself for its Divine Child's energy birth on December 21, 2082.

CHAPTER 27

CHANGING YOUR ENERGETIC DISPOSITION

"People will do anything, no matter how absurd, to stop
from facing their souls."
Carl Jung (1875–1961)

WHEN SURVIVALIST MAN FIRST appeared on the
planet 3.2 million years ago their energetic disposition
was always wired for survival in the physical realm. To
survive they needed to have an energetic disposition
of mind-body-soul. It was only through this that they
were able to survive.

Ever since consciousness man first appeared on
the planet 6000 years ago (in Eden) their energetic
disposition has also been wired for survival in
the physical realm exactly as survivalist man was.
However, in Higher Consciousness' seventh master

force consciousness man's energetic disposition is meant to evolve to soul-body-mind. However, because of Lucifer's betrayal this has not been allowed to happen because of EGO.

If we continue to be limited to our survival energetic disposition of mind-body-soul, Higher Consciousness has a zero chance of completing the Divine Child's energy birth on December 21, 2082. EGO has made this wisdom illogical, irrational and impossible to comprehend.

When your energetic disposition begins to change, your mind will gradually transition out of its consciousness limitations into your sub-consciousness, unconsciousness and collective unconsciousness memories and wisdoms. In Higher Consciousness' seventh master force, this is mankind's next giant leap forward.

All final life experience souls know through their life contract they agreed to before entering the physical realm, that this life experience is different than all others. No final-life experience soul is here to experience another passive, silent role; it is here to complete its lead starring role and lifelong evolution which can only begin by first changing your energetic disposition to soul-body-mind after awakening.

Physically, the soul was first discovered by the Swedish scientist, philosopher and theologian Emanuel Swedenborg (1688-1742) around 1742. His manuscript regarding this finding was not published until 1877. He referred to it as "spirituous lymph."

Studies have since determined the soul has mass. In 1907 Dr. Duncan MacDougall, an early twentieth century physician from Haverhill, Massachusetts, weighed six patients who were in the process of dying from tuberculosis. He discovered within minutes after their death, they had an unexplained average weight loss of 21 grams. MacDougall determined this was the average weight of the soul.

In 1988, a noetic science experiment studied the phenomenon of the soul's weight using more sophisticated tools. They performed experiments on 200 terminally ill patients, using a weighing devise that has a margin of error of less than 1/100,000 of an ounce. Their experiments showed that at the death of each patient, their weight loss was exactly 1/3000 of an ounce.

My 20 year Higher Consciousness internship further inspired me that souls fall into one of six soul age groups. They are: old souls, mature souls, middle-aged souls, adolescent souls, infant souls and young souls.

Today's 7.5 billion souls create a bell curve of soul ages. Old souls make up 2.5 per cent of our population. Mature souls make up 13.5 per cent of our population. Middle-aged souls make up 34 per cent of our population. Adolescent souls make up 34 per cent of our population. Infant souls make up 13.5 per cent of our population and young souls make up the final 2.5 per cent of our population.

A BELL CURVE

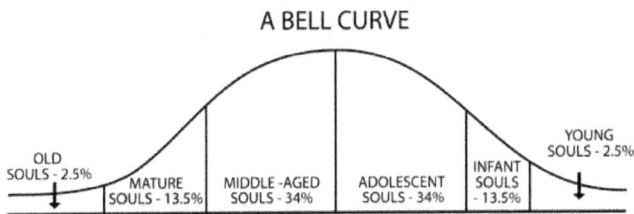

OLD SOULS - 2.5%
MATURE SOULS - 13.5%
MIDDLE-AGED SOULS - 34%
ADOLESCENT SOULS - 34%
INFANT SOULS - 13.5%
YOUNG SOULS - 2.5%

Old souls are the souls who will awaken first because they have the most hope of any soul group due to their many life experiences. They are also the first who will change their energetic disposition to soul-body-mind. Their subatomic strong force of nature gluon particle energy is made up of blue gluon particles. Their hope allows them to trust their soul and take greater risks than all other soul groups. The more an old soul hears the energetic wisdoms of its soul; the more awakened they become. Old souls will begin to awaken from their soul's energetic slumber first. It is the old souls who will be deified first. Old souls accept wisdom the fastest because they have crossed out of the physical realm into the afterlife divine realm - more than any other soul age group. Old souls have greater soul awareness, and are more in tune with their soul's communications.

Mature souls will be the early adaptors of their soul's wisdom. Their subatomic strong force of nature gluon particle energy also consists of blue gluon particle energy. Mature souls will not sense their soul's awakening as quickly as old souls but they will be involved early in the deification process. Mature souls will accept their soul's awakening because their souls have also crossed out of the physical realm into the afterlife divine realm many times and can also quickly sense their soul's communications.

The younger the soul is in its early physical realm life experiences, the less these souls are able to override their limitations of consciousness. The subatomic gluon particles of younger soul's atoms is red. These will be the ones that no matter how hard a person works with them regarding Higher Consciousness it will be much harder to sink in because their soul is not ready to awaken and override the energy of their mind because they are usually not in their soul's final-life experience. They are the ones who are easy to spot as they are motivated by dollars and cents. This is the soul age of Lucifer's *illuminati*.

First time souls have no hope and very little ability to comprehend the existence of their soul. The worst of first time souls manifest their behavior as psychopaths and sociopaths in a selfish and usually destructive way against society.

To access the energy that reveals the age group of a person's soul; simply engage another in a meaningful conversation. The more meaningful and deeper the conversation is, the older that person's soul is. Always look intently into a person's eyes and listen to how and what they are saying. The younger the soul, the tougher it will be for them to even make eye contact. Also, when verbal responses are only surface chitchat about the weather (or some other trivial topic) the younger the soul tends to be. Conversely, the deeper the responses of others mean they are more confident because their souls are older.

The eyes are the windows to the soul. Older souls radiate incredible amounts of light and energy through their eyes and their foreheads tend to glisten and radiate. The oldest of the old souls constantly radiate a comforting energy from their eyes much like that of a newborn. Older souls are also able to engage the eyes of others directly in conversation and have surrounded themselves with a strong support system of love.

Dogs and children are also attracted to older souls, and tend to have fewer interactions with younger souls. Dogs have been known to bark uncontrollably at younger souls.

During my 20 year Higher Consciousness internship I interviewed about 100 people who experienced a near death. The purpose was to understand what happened to them when their soul left their body during their near death experience.

Amazingly, everyone I interviewed had the same initial experience as his or her soul left their body and transcended into the afterlife divine realm. Everyone told me that when they died, their soul exited their body and hovered above it to review the circumstances of their body's death. Like myself when I died, my soul hovered at the ceiling of the emergency room looking down at my body. Everyone told me that when their soul was satisfied (regarding their death) it transcended out of the physical realm into the afterlife divine realm.

Most souls were greeted by comforting entities that they were familiar with upon arriving in the afterlife divine realm, for some it was a long lost relative and friend who had departed. For a few it was a religious figurehead and one gentleman from Philadelphia told me butterflies greeted him.

Approximately 75 per cent of my interviews were with women and 40 per cent of all deaths were by drowning. One of the most profound NDEs I encountered happened to Judy, whom I interviewed by telephone from California several years ago. Judy had been returning home to her farmhouse after grocery shopping on a sunny Saturday afternoon. When she got out of her car she saw her husband come out of the front door of their farmhouse frantically yelling and motioning her to immediately come into the house.

Judy left her groceries in the trunk of her car and went into the farmhouse. Her husband told her to go into the room that was to the right of the front door. Her two children were already there. They were visibly shaken and extremely emotional. After Judy had entered the room her husband slammed the door shut behind him. At that moment he pulled out a gun and shot Judy. Judy immediately died; her soul left her body and floated to the top of the room. Judy's soul witnessed her husband fatally shoot their two children and then kill himself. Judy's soul then left the farmhouse and transcended to the afterlife divine realm.

In my interviews I found that everyone had a completely different afterlife divine realm experience that was very personal to them. However, everyone agreed they didn't want to transcend back into their bodies after they had died. I was inspired in my 20 year Higher Consciousness internship that the energy on the other side in the afterlife is what the soul resonates with because it is what the soul is.

There is no fear or negative energy in the afterlife divine realm only the energetic perfection and perfect love of Higher Consciousness. When mentioning this to those I interviewed, they all agreed that the energetic perfection and perfect love of Higher Consciousness was the energy their souls craved and desired. All agreed this energy does not contain any fear or negativity. It was because of this that no one wanted to return to their bodies after their death: everyone wanted to stay exactly where they were in the afterlife divine realm with Higher Consciousness. We all knew this is the energy our soul is. However, like me everyone was told they must return. For most, the driving force in their lives to this day is to understand, actualize and complete what it was they were downloaded with during their NDE by Higher Consciousness.

Every soul's past, passive limited role has forced it to only communicate itself through its Higher Consciousness' ten energetic wisdoms. They are love, hope, imagination, inspiration, instinct, intuition, insight, coincidence, discernment and déjà vu. This has always been the soul's only way to communicate with the body and mind in all of its past life experiences. Therefore, our energetic disposition of mind-body-soul has provided us with only the energy to survive but not with the energy to thrive and unleash the deification of Higher Consciousness to complete our soul's evolution.

Don't ever think you're reading this book by accident. Everyone's final soul life experience is to unleash its lead, starring role and Higher Consciousness energetic perfection, perfect love and hope. This will conclude Higher Consciousness' seventh master force intent.

Due to Higher Consciousness' seventh master force unleashing the flesh of all final-life experience souls is not just limited to the physical realm for a finite period of time as it has always been, it has the potential to live forever. In order for anyone's flesh to ascend from its present physical realm limitations to its immortal state on Higher Consciousness' Divine Child their soul must complete its evolution by first becoming your lead energy. It is only through your soul becoming your lead energy that your flesh can transfigure into its thrive mode out of its survival mode.

During your soul's 6000 years of past life experiences Higher Consciousness studied and learned the energetic subtleties of EGO in order to help your soul complete its final-life experience evolution. The completion of your soul's final-life experience evolution happens through the incarnation of Higher Consciousness into your flesh which deifies you into the divine so that Higher Consciousness Divine Child can be born. Without at least 144,000 deified final life experience souls, Higher Consciousness' Divine Child will not have the required energy to sustain itself.

In all souls past life experiences "gut feelings" let the person know when something was right for them or when to beware of something that was not right for them. Because this is your soul's final-life experience, your gut feelings will be magnified and undeniable. Gut feelings is how your soul's awakening will be felt. Gut feelings never harm you or lead you astray as their only intent is to complete your soul's evolution by having Higher Consciousness incarnate into you and subatomically unleash its energetic perfection and perfect love into every atom of your being.

What has changed for your soul in this its final-life experience is that the "outside help" of Higher Consciousness it has always known was going to come is here.

Wisdom is Higher Consciousness' language that can only be comprehended by your soul. Lucifer, EGO and the mind cannot comprehend wisdom. Wisdom is Higher Consciousness' divine communication that the mind cannot perceive. Conversely, the soul does not resonate with Lucifer's lower red, green and blue energy of facts and knowledge that the mind resonates with.

The soul is the most powerful component of who you are. Not only does the soul provide the energy for your flesh to survive; it is Higher Consciousness.

Lucifer wants every mind to remain locked in his energetic mind prison of limitation until December 21, 2082 which would extinguish Higher Consciousness.

For some this maybe your "ah-ah" moment, as your energetic reason for being has now been understood. It probably doesn't jive with your consciousness limitations that have brought you to the point where you are at right now, living life on a day-by-day, second-by-second survival gangplank, which has always been what Lucifer has wanted. Your mind-body-soul consciousness energetic disposition cannot unleash your ultimate thrive energetic disposition and divine Higher Consciousness. It cannot unlock your infinite wealth potential, your infinite wisdom potential or your infinite wellness potential which are all attributes of Higher Consciousness seventh master force.

Every life experience your soul has ever had was to glean the wisdom it would require to conclude its soul evolution through you in this its final life experience.

For 6000 years your soul has waited for Higher

Consciousness' energy pregnancy secret and deification process thoughts to be made known.

Experts everywhere agree that no one has accessed more than five per cent of their mind's potential. As a result everyone tends to over-think and make lower quality decisions. This is the primary reason why teachers tell students to go with their first instinct. The more time spent thinking about the answer the greater the probability it is wrong. Unleashing your divine Higher Consciousness infinite potentials not only extinguishes EGO it will also reduce wrong decisions. As the mind goes deeper and moves out of its consciousness limitations; the better your decision-making becomes.

It is only through your soul's awakening that your energetic disposition can change.

Your soul has waited many life experiences to garner the respect and appreciation it has always deserved. Your soul's lifetimes of humiliation and bullying by Lucifer are about to end because of your new soul-body-mind energetic disposition.

CHAPTER 28

HIGHER CONSCIOUSNESS ACTIVATIONS

BY NOW MANY FINAL-LIFE EXPERIENCE souls will be awakening with gut feelings of excitement, inspiration and hope because of Higher Consciousness' energetic proximity to your soul. Some may be awakening to the feelings of shock and anger because of what Lucifer and EGO have kept hidden from you. Whatever your gut feelings may be; they are the gut feelings your soul has been waiting to unleash to you. The awakening of your soul and energetic disposition change is the pre-requisite that will allow your mind to escape Lucifer's energetic mind prison of consciousness limitation.

If you're not here yet, and if this truly is your soul's final-life experience, this chapter will certainly help.

After many lifetimes of silence, your soul's long-awaited awakening will begin. This is the destiny and final evolutionary step of mankind. It is meant to dispose your mind of its male survivalist limitations of consciousness and replace it with your Higher Consciousness female thrive infinite potentials. The incarnation of Higher Consciousness is not compatible with the dull male, consciousness limitations, survivalist mindset and EGO.

After completing your Higher Consciousness deification process pre-requisites of soul awakening and energetic disposition your Higher Consciousness incarnation can begin with your Higher Consciousness Activations (HCA). HCAs are how your soul energetically re-activates itself again with Higher Consciousness. This meet up is exactly like your soul has always had - except this time it is in the physical realm while you are alive and not in the divine realm after the body your soul was in died. It is your Moses Mount Sinai experience. Unlike every past life your soul has ever had, this time you (your flesh) will not have to die in order for your soul to be re-activated with Higher Consciousness.

 HCAs are Higher Consciousness' re-activation with your soul in the physical realm that have always been intended for consciousness man. Six thousand years ago, the first HCAs were meant to have been with Adam and Eve: who would have shared their deification process wisdom of HCA's with their offspring who would have done the same with their offspring and so on and so on.

Higher Consciousness' seventh master force was originally intended to be unleashed this way 6000 years ago. However, because of Lucifer's betrayal, it had to be delayed until the unveiling of Higher Consciousness' energy pregnancy secret and deification process thoughts which also was meant to have been revealed 6000 years ago. HCA's convert your soul from its isolated passive, silent role into its lead starring role to begin mankind's final evolutionary step that completes their evolution.

Your soul has gone through all of its previous life experiences in order to prepare itself for this pinnacle life experience to unleash its freedom, purpose and evolution. Your soul's reactivation with Higher Consciousness energetically transforms it from being an unattached single angel energy thread into its energetic totality of Higher Consciousness energetic perfection, perfect love and hope. It restores your soul to its complete energetic dignity and glory it was before the beginning of time.

Because of Lucifer's betrayal up until now in the physical realm it has only been the souls of Moses and Jesus that have unlocked their absolute Higher Consciousness dignity and glory.

Concluding your Higher Consciousness' seventh master force intent deifies you into the Divine as it has always meant to do. Higher Consciousness' energy pregnancy can begin when at least 144,000 have been incarnated by Higher Consciousness which guarantees its Divine Child birth.

Many have told me that the completion of their HCAs was the best thing they have ever done. I have had the privilege to lead many through their HCAs to reactivate their soul with Higher Consciousness. HCAs are always completed at one's leisure in their private domain over telephone or Skype.

To begin, one's HCAs your mind must be slowed down to its Theta brainwave rhythm speed. Your Theta brainwave rhythm speed operates at 4 to 8 cycles per second. This is the brainwave rhythm speed your collective unconsciousness and soul can discern the divine communications of Higher Consciousness at. It is only through your Theta brainwave rhythm speeds that you are able to understand the communications of Higher Consciousness.

HCAs are guided out of body experiences for your soul. They take your soul to meet Higher Consciousness as it has always done except this time you do not need to die for your soul to experience this. HCAs access the deepest recesses of your soul's mind which is your collective unconsciousness.

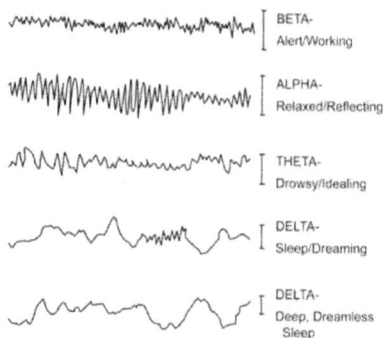

BETA-
Alert/Working

ALPHA-
Relaxed/Reflecting

THETA-
Drowsy/Idealing

DELTA-
Sleep/Dreaming

DELTA-
Deep, Dreamless
Sleep

Brainwave Speeds
1. Beta – 14-39 cycles per second.
2. Alpha – 8-14 cycles per second.
3. Theta – 4-8 cycles per second.
4. Delta – 0-4 cycles per second.

Your Theta brainwave rhythm speed is the energetic channel that dials into the energetic communications of Higher Consciousness. It is only your Theta brainwave rhythm speeds that can discern Higher Consciousness' attempt to re-connect with your soul. Lucifer and EGO do not have the ability to access this communication. Your Theta brainwave rhythm communication will produce a definite and indisputable impression on you. It is like nothing you have ever experienced before; it will take you into hidden energetic dimensions of your collective unconsciousness that you have not previously tapped into.

Your Theta brainwave speed is different from your Beta brainwave rhythm speed. Your Beta brainwave speed is your mind's brainwave rhythm speed which your consciousness comprehends daily life at. It operates at 14 to 39 cycles per second. This speed cannot comprehend the divine communications of Higher Consciousness.

Some benefits (as shared by clients) are:

1. Develop a greater awareness of reality;
2. Confirm their physical immortality;
3. Unleash their infinite potentials they didn't know existed;
4. Unleash the perfect love, ultra-positivity and infinite potential of Higher Consciousness within them;
5. Unleash the energetic perfection, perfect love and hope of Higher Consciousness' seventh master force into their daily life;
6. Escape from their energetic mind prison and debt sentence;
7. Eliminate the fear of death,

8. Unleash their Higher Consciousness potentials (to be revealed later);
9. Increase their desire for life;
10. Activate their legacy in life;
11. Reveal their energetic role and purpose in life;
12. Unleash their spontaneous healing;
13. Maximize their self-awareness;
14. Maximize their enlightenment;
15. Recognize and understand their past lives;
16. Understand their between lives downloads from their previous life experiences in the afterlife divine realm;
17. Maximize their energetic transfiguration into the divine Higher Consciousness;
18. Increase their self-respect;
19. Eliminate pain, fear and insecurity;
20. Maximize wisdom;
21. Accesses their all-knowingness of everything;
22. Increase energy;
23. Unleash past unknown memories;
24. Complete and fulfills their life;
25. Unleash a monetary wealth potential that most never thought was possible.

During your HCAs there is no gravitational force to hold your soul down; no sense of time to break up your soul's reactivation with Higher Consciousness and no physical sensations. You feel no pain, temperature, or fatigue as your soul is simply led to reactivate with Higher Consciousness.

Most HCAs encounter other soul fragments of who they were in past lives that have become blocked and stuck in their energetic travels and journey back to Higher Consciousness. These identities are energies from past lives that must be set free. Many times clients have experienced profound improvements to their health when these soul fragment identities are released. Some have met loved ones who have passed away. Some have met historical figures: and no two HCAs are the same.

HCAs are always easier the earlier they are completed in one's life.

Everyone has a soul age which can be vastly different than your chronological age. Today there are many younger individuals who are older souls who easily access their childlike innocence of exploration and discovery during their HCAs.

Conversely there are older individuals that are younger souls. They tend to be well entrenched in their minds' energetic mind prisons and for the most part lack hope. Unfortunately most younger souls are not in their soul's final-life experience.

I have met (chronologically) young individuals who are energetically old souls and chronologically elderly individuals who are young souls. There is absolutely no rhythm or reason to the age of your soul other than it just is.

Here is a copy of an email I received from Mike after the first HCA session I had with him.

I felt my body start to lift off the bed moving to the right side of me then hovering about one foot above the bed at the level of the light. I saw the light turn into what looked like the center of the galaxy with bright striations emanating all over. At that point my hands became tight and started vibrating as if a power surge was going through them. I then began to feel extremely warm ... when I opened my eyes then closed them again I saw what looked like the photo negative of everything in the room including myself and for a brief moment I could even see the skeletal bones in my hands and arms as if I was looking at an X-ray. I then felt a brief moment of peace and happiness come over me and I started to laugh as if on a drug (but not on a drug). I haven't felt like that for a long, long time.

Here is some email correspondence I received from Becky during the HCA sessions I had with her.

It began with the following email.

Hi JC,

Something has come to mind about that session.

Do you remember when I was at the chalkboard and I said, "I think it's a flower?" The reason I said "I think" is because of the way I drew it. Normally, I would draw a flower like the image of image A that I have attached to this email. But the way I drew it is as per the image of image B. Do you see the difference in the way the petals were drawn in these two images?

Image A: *Image B:*

In image A, the petals were drawn down and around. In image B, they were drawn up and then they cross down over themselves. This indicates that, when I'm teaching, my higher self takes over and directs the flow of information.

My response to her email was as follows.

This is profound. Thanks for sharing.

What I see in image B is you soaring and flying. The petals representing your head, arms and legs and are connected to your body. Your arms and legs are acting as your wings. This is an image of your deification into Higher Consciousness (like a flying turtle).

I must admit that the image you drew within the box on the board has been on my mind. This revelation you have given me about the flower has provided me with a possible missing element.

Let me know how this resonates with you.

Closing in the box around the images clearly closes off the message. I know the message is about you (and all of humanity).

When trying to comprehend what this means, I am impressed that the proper way to understand this is to read it like a pyramid, from the middle then to the left and then the right.

House represents your absolute security and absolute value.

The big heart is your physical realm absolute and represents the first half of the equation the soaring flower is your afterlife divine realm absolute and represents the second half of the equation.

So your drawings are speaking to me this way.

The complete you is secure, safe and valuable and is the answer to the equation of who Becky energetically is. For you to be your complete secure self it is the combination of your complete physical realm self that will produce the massive big heart, eliminate all fears and securities to unleash your physical realm purity and Higher Consciousness.

Your drawing is the equation of your deification into Higher Consciousness and also is your energetic absolutes of Higher Consciousness' energetic perfection, perfect love and hope.

Your drawing is energetically what we all are and our life energies, energetic freedom, purpose and potential for living this life experience.

From a mathematical perspective I am impressed this is our energetic formula of who we are. The formula is the following:

$.001 + 99.999 = 100.$

House is 100 or 100 per cent of energetic absolute of who we are and our ultimate genius potential (also all of humanity).

99.999 is the soaring flower or 99.999 per cent your HCA's produce. This is what lies beyond everyone's consciousness limitations.

Humanity has done life only accessing .001 per cent of their potential in the physical realm in their consciousness limitations.

It will be amazing as 100 per cent works together and unleashes the complete deification of Higher Consciousness as it was meant to be 6000 years ago.

Have you just seen the energetic pictogram for Higher Consciousness' deification process?

Thank you for sharing.

All HCA sessions begin with the removal of your physical realm energies. It is only your Theta brainwave rhythm speed that can access this state. If slowing your mind down to access your Theta brainwave rhythm speed is a problem, I have found that taking one tablespoon of liquid magnesium 30 minutes prior to the beginning of your HCA session will help to calm down your mind.

Clients who have completed their HCAs have told me it significantly enhanced their life. It provided the hope, meaning and purpose to their life many thought was impossible to access. Some have told me that it has left them speechless with new feelings and insights of bliss, love, freedom, abundance and wisdom that they didn't previously have. They have unlocked the door of Lucifer's energetic mind prison and no longer see the world through the energetic blinders they were wearing while stuck in Lucifer's energetic mind prison serving their debt sentence. Many found their

HCAs have unleashed new, specialized knowledge and wisdoms, which they had not previously known.

You can never go through your HCAs if you are afraid of new ideas, or if you suffer from indecision, doubt, worry, caution, procrastination or hoarding. You simply cannot communicate with Higher Consciousness with fear, doubt or negativity attached. This is Lucifer's energy and the energy Higher Consciousness must eliminate so it's Divine Child can be birthed.

There are some who at this moment are experiencing an undeniable fluttering explosion or bubbling up feeling inside of them as they read. If this is you, please know this is an energetic signal of joy and gut feeling coming from your soul as it begins to awaken. It is your soul letting you know it is ready to be reactivated again with Higher Consciousness to complete its evolution.

Activating Higher Consciousness' energetic perfection, perfect love and hope does not depend on anything except you. There are no favorites. Everyone's soul is an angelic energy thread of Higher Consciousness that has been eternally waiting for this moment so that its life mission can be completed.

As children, we do not separate the possible from the impossible. This is why the younger a person's mind is the older their soul tends to be and the easier it is to reactivate and unleash Higher Consciousness.

Science has proven energy cannot be destroyed. Hence, one's soul and angelic energy thread of Higher Consciousness never dies.

HCAs begin by removing any and all energetic

parasites and toxins that have caused energetic blockages in your soul. Cleansing your soul's energetic blockages is always the first step in your HCAs.

During your HCAs chances are you will encounter different allies, tests and enemies that have become stuck in your soul and need to be removed. HCAs have also encountered alien energies and enemies to this Universe that have entered your soul and need to be cleared. All foreign energies to your soul must be removed and cleared during your HCA and sent back to where they came from. Many HCAs also encounter allies and identities of who you were in previous life experiences that also must now be sent back to Higher Consciousness.

All these energies must be cleansed before your soul can re-activate with Higher Consciousness.

Many times your soul's allies, tests and enemies that are still stuck in your soul tend to manifest themselves in your daily life.

For some I have found that as they complete their HCAs, new people have just magically appeared to either help them complete their HCAs or deny them from completing their HCAs.

To understand what can happen during HCA sessions one of my clients (whom I shall call Beth) agreed for me to share her HCAs. Beth's HCAs took place over the telephone, while she was in the comfort of her home.

BETH'S HCA SESSION #1

Beth's first HCA session began when she eliminated all of her physical realm energies. I knew Beth was in her Theta brainwave rhythm speed state when she said, "The gates to hell are always open, and I'm stuck and cannot move on."

Beth's soul revealed a globe out of which different streams, bells, rings, markings and points were sticking out. She knew these points were different life experiences from her many previous life experiences.

I asked Beth to look around as she began to travel deeper and see if any past soul fragments from past life experiences could be found. She quickly found a soul fragment reveal itself to her as Angra, whose family had been wiped out in an invasion when she was 22 years of age. Men on horseback slaughtered Angra's husband and their baby's right before her eyes. This occurred during what she thought was the Mongol invasion.

Beth's past soul fragment of Angra was stuck in her soul. Due to the traumatic death she had experienced, and because of the loss of her husband and babies, Angra had trust issues with moving on. Ironically, Beth has constantly had trust issues manifest in her life as anguish, anger and sadness. I pointed Angra to the light of the afterlife divine realm, which she had been trying to enter. Angra saw it. As she looked into it she saw her husband and her babies in the light with their arms held open, they were calling her to come home. Beth saw Angra go through the light and death portal and leave her soul.

Beth then had Dungrith come forward. He was a man of the woods, who could not release himself. He said, "I killed him. I'm not worthy. I killed my brother over a woman." When Dungrith was pointed to the light, he saw the door was open and waiting for him. Beth also saw him leave and go through the light.

Beth then saw Jacob from Jamaica. Beth's voice then spoke to me with a thick Jamaican accent. Jacob lived with nature. A White man took him away on a boat; who then sank the boat. Jacob never saw his family again. Jacob felt abandoned, alone and discontented. He knew he didn't belong here but could not move on. Beth saw him leave quickly in a rocket, into the light.

This concluded Beth's first HCA session. The total time was two hours.

I have since made it a practice not to exceed 60-minute HCA sessions. They are simply too draining for the person experiencing them when they exceed 60 minutes.

BETH'S HCA SESSION #2

At Beth's second HCA session, she entered into her Theta brainwave rhythm state again where she saw a glowing golden globe. Her golden globe was blocked like water at the edge of a dam. She said, "Golden globe is stuck, cannot move down." Beth knew this was a huge issue. She felt resigned to the golden globe being stuck. I asked

Beth to watch the globe. As she watched, the globe became brighter. It appeared to be getting closer to her very quickly.

As the golden globe moved closer, she saw a man from a previous life experience. He revealed himself as Simon, a knight who had lived during the Dark Ages, before the Knights Templar. Simon revealed the code to an artifact that he had sworn to uphold. The artifact was part of a power that triggered DNA to yield instantaneous manifestations. The Sun was darkened as a result of Simon revealing this information. I pointed Simon toward the light, which overcame his guilt for disclosing this code.

Simon saw the light reaching out to him and he became "one" with it. He went into the light and was home. Beth felt goose bumps when Simon went home. She said everyone was happy he was home.

Beth is an old soul who has a lot of light. This has attracted forces from other energy cells who are monitoring her. When I asked Beth if there were any others coming forward from within her soul, a non-human entity appeared and identified itself as Sondra, from Planet 421. It said, "I am of a planet, not of this Universe." I asked Sondra how it had entered into the soul of Beth. I forcefully told the entity to leave Beth. Sondra said Beth invited her. Sondra said she and others had been using Beth to learn for the federation of planets. I asked Beth if she had sold her soul. Beth said she had only loaned her soul out. I had an intense battle with Sondra who didn't want to leave. After about fifteen minutes Sondra eventually left the soul of Beth.

I asked Beth to look around and look for other entities to reveal themselves. But none appeared. Beth was energetically exhausted after this session.

Later, I received the following email from Beth.

Wow JC!

That was pretty amazing. I feel sooooo happy. Like my chest is one big balloon of happy.

I would like to reside in this forever. Suddenly everything has no importance. No feelings of resentment or painful memories. Nothing feels like it is sticking. I feel like I am in a healing place drawing in a rest period so that I will be more ready when the time is right to begin working...whatever that looks like. I have a sense my life is going to be very exciting and I have no idea doing what...although I suspect I will be helping people clear their blocks and will be able to see them more clearly.

THANK YOU THANK YOU THANK YOU.

It is a wonderful thing that you do.

BETH'S HCA SESSION #3

Before we started Beth's third HCA session, she started to shake with excitement. Once she was in her Theta brainwave rhythm state, this session began when I asked her what she was seeing. Again she saw the golden globe; parts of which were moving like a river.

This confirmed once again that Beth was in her Theta brainwave rhythm state.

Then, Beth saw a very bright light, which was much closer to her than it had been before. Being close to the light, she felt joy, peace and happiness. But she knew she was not ready to go through the light. She said others were still trapped.

The next soul fragment that came forward identified himself as Luke. He was from the year 1789, the time of the Spanish explorers. Luke had explored down the east coast and in inlets, looking for gold. He was unable to return, became shipwrecked and died. He had been sleeping in a room and was suddenly trapped, there was water everywhere and he could not get out. He couldn't breathe.

Because he was scared, Luke could not go through the light. He didn't want to go into the light. But when I told him to look up at the light, he was able to move into it very quickly. When he passed through the light, he was greeted by two voices that both Beth and myself audibly heard greet him.

Next, Beth saw Joshua who was known as Nick. Nick was a 10-year-old crippled boy who had been murdered and was confused. After much delay, I was led to tell him what had taken place during his life was not his fault. He said he should have listened and not gone into the darkness. When I told him to go to the light, he went through it.

Beth's soul now confirmed to her that she didn't have any more soul fragments or invaders stuck in her soul. I then instructed Beth to move forward into the light, which she did.

Through the light Beth saw miles and miles of amazing, flower-filled landscape. She sat down on a cliff, far removed from anything and everyone.

She immediately saw her old, English sheepdog Benji, whom she had missed very much. He was happy and full of energy. Together, they began walking toward a group of people.

Then Beth saw a young girl. When Beth asked the young girl who she was, she was told she was the daughter she didn't have: the daughter who didn't live. She told Beth she was fine, but the energetic circumstances were not right for her to enter the physical realm. This gave Beth tremendous peace as she had always held this traumatic experience close to her heart. She had been punishing herself for many years for her failure to deliver this child.

Benji and Beth began walking toward a village where many of her friends and relatives were waiting for her. These people included her parents, her grandparents and her uncle; all were happy and proud of her for making it here while still being alive. Everyone acknowledged her and encouraged her for what she was doing.

Suddenly, the sky was golden, the trees were like a tapestry, music was everywhere and there wasn't any blackness. She heard a voice. We waited for about 10 minutes. But no one came. Then she saw flowers everywhere. She knew the flowers were the energy from

Higher Consciousness. They said, "I am Higher Consciousness. The only plan for you is with me."

The total time was two hours. Beth sent me the following message the day after her third HCA session.

Hello JC,

These are just thoughts which have come to me in the aftermath of our session...

The two aspects...one which died in a shipwreck (Luke?) and (Joshua/Nick) both of these died with lung

issues. Luke by drowning and Nick with a knife to the chest. I am wondering if my breathing will get easier with their release. I also found that I actually felt a physical evacuation when they left, like a movement of energy being pulled out of the physical body.

Am also somewhat annoyed about Benji, the dog. I have cried over that stupid dog more times than anyone else in my life. I mourn him over and over and it doesn't seem to finish...although it gets further away with time.

Whenever I see an old English sheepdog, I just turn to fluff and think about him. I guess he is the closest thing (or the real thing) to unconditional love I have ever had in this lifetime.

I had a very wakeful night last night, as I was high on energy.

You will see a picture of my Benji attached. He was big, fluffy and very sweet!

Thank you again, I appreciate it VERY MUCH!
Beth

Beth's dog Benji.

BETH'S HCA SESSION #4

To begin Beth's fourth HCA session, she entered into her Theta brainwave rhythm speed. At this time, she heard sounds, like a hum and heartbeat. Then she went through the light and saw a city near the bottom of a hill. The city was crystal and bright.

Sounds were coming from it. Beth saw it to be magnificent and beautiful. The crystal had many colors. Within the city was one main building that had glass and marble in front of it. She was amazed at the art patterns in the rock. The patterns were making sounds as if they were alive. She pushed down on a handle on the door of the building and walked inside.

The inside of the building was as bright as it was outside. The light was emanating from the pure energetic perfection and perfect love of Higher Consciousness. Beth felt honored to be in this presence. She was very happy to be with the energetic perfection and perfect love of Higher Consciousness. Next, she was led to a room that was bare. Beth felt it to be a place of worship. There were 11 men in this room, four of whom were sitting on the floor. There was nothing else in this room; it didn't need anything else. She was told that few arrive here while being alive in the physical realm, she was on a long journey and this was a stepping-stone in her journey.

Now Beth's soul entered its deepest stage. She felt an awareness she had not felt before. She was told it would increase her vibrations and her consciousness. She was told to call certain people forward into a group to activate and unleash their souls. She was told she needed to be cleared and prepared to go forward and help support those in this regard.

At this point, I was impressed it was time to reactivate Beth's soul with Higher Consciousness. After her soul's Higher Consciousness re-activation Beth was immediately impressed this meant profound events were about to unfold in her life. She was ready to open and reveal incredible synchronicity through Higher Consciousness. Beth indicated this was all she wanted to do and this is why she is alive today. She has no will but to do what Higher Consciousness desires for her life.

Beth then found herself in a courtyard where a man approached her from the courtyard gates. He was dressed in attire from biblical times. Beth noticed she was dressed the same way. The man greeted her as an old friend and told her a group of people had been waiting for her and had agreed to come forward. Then the group surrounded her. The man reminded Beth it must become her priority to dissolve her ego and this must occur before more events can be revealed to her. It was further revealed to her that this experience awaits everyone and will impact all of humanity. This is not a task, but rather a quest. The initiative produces the outcome.

The total time for this HCA session was two hours.

To this day I continue to assist Beth in completing her Higher Consciousness deification process.

It became apparent to me during my 20 year Higher Consciousness internship while working with clients during their HCAs, that prior to their HCA completion they had no idea of what their true potential in life was meant to be either physically, emotionally, mentally, spiritually, relationally or financially. This is because no one had ever reactivated their soul with Higher Consciousness in the physical realm before.

It is amazing how Higher Consciousness begins to work after its re-activation with the soul. After helping many complete their HCAs I have had the honor to help many complete their Higher Consciousness deification process. I have noticed that it always begins to expand one's "love bubble." Love bubbles are a person's bubble of love where their giving and receiving of love resides.

I have heard many times from clients that their love bubbles have grown to heights they never could have imagined. Some have told me their love bubbles have expanded their sexual experiences. They have shared with me that their lovemaking has become more meaningful, fulfilling and frequent. One client told me he is able to please his wife in ways he was never able to do before because now he is able to intuitively feel and satisfy her needs and pleasures simply because he can intuitively sense them which is something he never was able to do prior to completing his HCA's.

Many clients have told me their relationships with spouses, family, friends and others has improved because they are no longer in their "box of self" and can now actually feel others by actually hearing what their saying. Others have expressed a feeling of euphoria for life that they never had before. Some have even added a personal fitness program to their schedule for the first time in their life and a couple clients were immediately impressed to cut sugar from their diet and have lost incredible amounts of weight for the first time in their lives.

Unquestionably, the biggest change clients have noticed is an increase to their energy; life does not appear to be the sluggish challenge that it once was. If anyone suffers from low energy it is because your soul is leaving your body. No one lacks energy when their soul fully charges their atoms subatomic strong nuclear force.

I have found that clients have begun to experience energy in different ways as well. Some have suddenly begun to see multi-dimensional energy and auras around life similar to Kirlian photography.

HUMAN ENERGY AS SEEN THROUGH KIRLIAN PHOTOGRAPHY

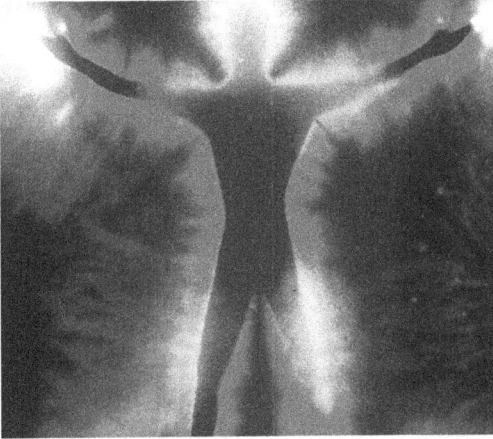

Some have mentioned they have begun to see multi-dimensional energy in the air, where previously nothing was seen before. Some have told me they are able to see the colors of multi-dimensional energy actually move in and out of the minds of people, while others have picked up the vibrations of energy from living objects. Some have been able to energetically pick up the thoughts of others and know what a person is going to say and do before they do it. Some even noticed an enhanced sense of touch as they feel multi-dimensional energy in a way, which is totally new to anything they have previously felt. Most clients report back that their dreams have become more meaningful, real and profound.

Up until now, Higher Consciousness has only incarnated itself twice in the physical realm to Moses and Jesus. They are also the only two that have ever had their flesh's sub atomic strong nuclear force deified to ascend.

However, there was a time in the life of Moses when his soul had not reactivated with Higher Consciousness. Energetically his Beta state of consciousness was no different than where your Beta state of consciousness is at today. Like all of us, Moses needed to complete his HCAs before his soul could reactivate with Higher Consciousness.

Your soul's evolution cannot be fulfilled unless your HCAs are completed. Your deification process cannot be realized unless your HCAs are completed. However, most importantly Higher Consciousness' Divine Child energy birth cannot take place unless they are completed.

Higher Consciousness needs you to complete your HCA's!

CHAPTER 29

THE REWARD OF HIGHER CONSCIOUSNESS

"Energy cannot be created or destroyed. It can only be
changed from one form to another."
Albert Einstein (1879–1955)

BY COMPLETING YOUR HCAs, your soul and Higher
Consciousness will be "one" again.

Energetically, Higher Consciousness can now begin
to incarnate itself subatomically into every one of your
atoms after Lucifer's EGO has been removed from your
mind.

Lucifer's betrayal forced Higher Consciousness' final
energy apocalypse to be in your mind. This apocalypse
is your Energetic Battle of Armageddon (EBA). It is
Higher Consciousness' planned energetic cataclysm
that must remove EGO, Lucifer and all Luciferin fear
and negative energy from your mind. It begins once

your HCA's are completed.

Originally in Higher Consciousness' seventh master force, consciousness man was not supposed to experience any EBA. Higher Consciousness was not supposed to have any apocalypses because Lucifer's betrayal was never supposed to have happened. Jesus was never even supposed to be. However, because of Lucifer's betrayal all of this must be.

Every final-life experience soul joyfully waits for its energetic disposition change to soul-body-mind and your flesh's incarnation into Higher Consciousness.

When Higher Consciousness incarnates it becomes your ultimate force carrier as through its weak force of nature (unleashed at the opening of its fourth master force 13.75 billion years ago) it will cause Lucifer's EGO to decay. Lucifer's EGO decay will be a subatomic disintegration of itself by Higher Consciousness at distances of less than 0.0001 per cent of the diameter of a proton. Science refers to this interaction as quantum flavor dynamics.

It will bring on your restoring force trials. To consciousness, a restoring force is a force that gives rise to a physical systems equilibrium. If a physical system, like our flesh, is perturbed away from its equilibrium (as Lucifer and EGO have done) its restoring force can bring our flesh back to its equilibrium. Welcome and understand your restoring force trials. They are Lucifer's final attempt to bring your consciousness back to his Luciferin equilibrium of limitations.

Beware, as Lucifer may use others in his restoring force trials against you. Others might find your

Higher Consciousness deification process and "call to freedom" threatening because either they are not a final-life experience soul or they are energetically paralyzed by money or they have selfish motives that your incarnation into Higher Consciousness will take away from them. Lucifer will not be shy about using others as your restoring force trials are meant to turn your Higher Consciousness deification off.; his very survival depends up on it. Lucifer's major means to of restoring force trials is always through his drug of money.

At this point, after completing your HCAs you be keenly aware of others' energy. As much as it may hurt, during this critical time it is possible that you will temporarily need to break your association with some of your closest ties who are led by Lucifer's fear and negativity energy until your deification is complete.

Feelings are your energetic barometer, they measure energy. It is imperative not to cave into these energetic pressures that deny you from completing your deification. Lucifer will be agitated and vigorously unleash his major weapons of fear, negativity and money against you. Thanks to Lucifer, your restoring force trials must be completed before you can experience your complete Higher Consciousness reward.

At this point of your deification the door of your energetic mind prison has now been unlocked and opened. You cannot allow it to be closed again with you still trapped inside. Trapping yourself back in Lucifer's energetic mind prison would be akin to committing your energetic suicide - which is

Lucifer's goal. Your chances of escape would then be impossible; Lucifer would have been alerted to your intentions and will place his energetic correction officers outside of your energetic mind prison cell to ensure you never escape.

The strength of your character is about to be taxed like never before. Your EBA's purpose is to defeat EGO. EBAs can last a few minutes or many years. They will all be completed by December 21, 2082. The quicker an EBA is completed the longer your Higher Consciousness reward in the physical realm will last.

Lucifer has forced everyone's EBA. They are everyone's "Get out of jail card." They are for everyone to escape their energetic mind prison of limitation and go beyond their consciousness limits.

For some they may feel a sense of panic as they journey into the unknown; however, for most they will feel a sense of relief knowing they have left behind their limitations to embark on their reason for being. Lucifer's primary way of impacting you will always be through money. Money is his drug that he knows he cannot lose control of.

As your EBA intensifies, your world might change in a way you may not have anticipated. Do not let it produce panic or anxiety. Through EGO and stress Lucifer may try to energetically numb you and make you afraid of your pending change. For many they will encounter changes to their personal life that could cause a short term uncomfortable feel.

All Luciferian valleys are short term as evidenced by Lucifer's temptation of Jesus in the wilderness 2000 years ago. This encounter happened only 30 years after Higher Consciousness had cut all of its energy ties with Lucifer. Jesus was Higher Consciousness' left eye energy replacement of Lucifer. Lucifer was energetically stronger back then than he is today; yet, he could only muster a feeble attack against Jesus.

Today, 2000 years later Lucifer is energetically much weaker and his energy testing for most will be much less then Jesus' because none of us carry the energetic significance to Higher Consciousness that Jesus had because none of us are its left eye energy. Yes, our soul is an angel energy thread of Higher Consciousness third eye, but, it is not a complete energy eye and lampstand as Jesus and Lucy are. Therefore, like Jesus you must stand firm and deny Lucifer of his testing so that Higher Consciousness can remove EGO from your mind.

For everyone the significance of their consciousness attachments will change after their HCA. You will now be able to easily categorize them as essential or non-essential (journals are recommended to document this).

An increased awareness of maintaining your essential consciousness attachments will be revealed and an increased focus on divesting yourself of your non-essential consciousness attachments will also be revealed. Essential and non-essential consciousness attachments will vary on a person-by-person basis. Something that may be essential to you might not be essential to someone else.

To the mind, Lucifer will try and make this appear to be irrational because it directly attacks his significance and intent of money.

As your EBA intensifies Higher Consciousness will open up your subconscious, unconsciousness and collective unconsciousness memories to flood and overwhelm EGO. This will be something Lucifer has never dealt with before.

Your subconscious is where every five-sense sensation, feeling and memory you have ever experienced in your life is stored. It is where your body and mind life memories are kept. When unleashed, it will help make you less rigid and energetically younger. Your unconsciousness and collective unconsciousness feelings are Higher Consciousness' energetic perfection, perfect love and hope that Lucifer has denied you of while he has kept you in his energetic mind prison.

With these memories unleashed, you will have reached your EBA summit. This will be the moment in time when your EBA decision will be made to either accept or deny Higher Consciousness. This was the same point that your mind would have come to 6000 years ago except EGO would not have been involved and no restoring force trials would have been needed. Will you choose to authorize Higher Consciousness to complete your deification process and have EGO extinguished or will you choose to keep EGO? Only you can decide what is best for you.

Very rarely will a person get to this point with just one limitation or regret in their life. Usually one is brought here by a series of life events that have taken place. All final-life experience souls will be brought to this point; however, as prescribed in Higher Consciousness' seventh master force, it must be your free will choice that authorizes EGO to be extinguished.

If your EBA decision is to extinguish EGO, it will lead to unleashing your Higher Consciousness reward for yourself with the elimination of Lucifer, EGO and all energy of fear and negativity from your mind. This is when Higher Consciousness' incarnation of energetic perfection perfect love and hope seventh master force attributes becomes the energy of your mind as it has always meant to be.

You will now begin to understand and see yourself in an entirely different light because of your mind's Higher Consciousness incarnation of energetic perfection, perfect love and hope seventh master force energy attributes that have become your mind's new energy force. Your mind will begin to accept its magnificence, which it never knew before while trapped in Lucifer's energetic mind prison. For your mind, knowing that all its wear and tear, pain, suffering and negative experiences is about to end is priceless.

When EGO is defeated and rendered powerless your mind is brought to Higher Consciousness' energetic ground-zero point where it was meant to have been 6000 years ago.

Once here it will allow Higher Consciousness's incarnation to unleash its rewards, which you were always meant to have.

First will be the outpouring of Higher Consciousness' energetic perfection attributes subatomically to your flesh's atoms. Now without EGO, Higher

Consciousness' energetic perfection attribute and your infinite wellness potential will be unleashed subatomically to all of your flesh's atoms as was intended 6000 years ago. Unfortunately EGO has denied this and manifested disease, pain, stress and aging that has hastened all of consciousness man's premature death for 6000 years.

Next will be the outpouring of Higher Consciousness' perfect love attribute and your infinite wisdom potential. This Higher Consciousness "at-one-ment" enhances all of your five senses and unlocks your sixth and seventh senses of divine Higher Consciousness wisdom that has been placed within you.

Finally will be the outpouring of Higher Consciousness' hope attribute and your infinite monetary wealth potential. This Higher Consciousness attribute has needed to be added by Higher Consciousness because of Lucifer's betrayal. Higher Consciousness must become the dominant energy of money. It must eliminate Lucifer completely as the energy behind money and extinguish all fear and negativity in order to birth its Divine Child. Your infinite monetary wealth potential must happen so Higher Consciousness can become money's dominate energy force.

Higher Consciousness' incarnation must be completed in at least 144,000 in order to birth Higher Consciousness' Divine Child on December 21, 2082.

Higher Consciousness' deification process is its energy portal that unleashes you from your ordinary world of limitations. It is the portal to your infinite potentials and physical immortality that lie beyond your consciousness limitations to complete your soul's evolution.

Higher Consciousness' reward energetically purifies and cleanses you with its energetic perfection, perfect love and hope as you do life in your souls Higher Consciousness deification zone as your soul has always intended for its final life experience.

Higher Consciousness' reward energetically transcends you into Higher Consciousness. Your energetic perfection, perfect love and hope divine Higher Consciousness is the only energetic sustenance that Higher Consciousness' Divine Child can be.

Your Higher Consciousness deification zone delivers you to your Higher Consciousness divine glorification of energetic perfection and perfect love. There isn't any Luciferian decay, destruction and death here; only your infinite wisdom, infinite wealth and infinite wellness.

CHAPTER 30

YOUR HIGHER CONSCIOUSNESS REWARD

WITH LUCIFER DEFEATED AND EGO extinguished from your mind, Higher Consciousness can now complete its incarnation of you as it was meant to be 6000 years ago.

Old consciousness limitations will begin to disappear as you move beyond your consciousness limitations. Your soul will have moved past its physical realm isolation into its energetic totality as Higher Consciousness.

With your mind released from its energetic mind prison and your soul's at-one-ment with Higher Consciousness, Higher Consciousness can now begin to unleash its infinite potentials. It will energetically begin to transfigure your flesh's temporary red, green and blue subatomic strong nuclear force gluons to its divine permanent violet strong nuclear force gluons. This is its energetic perfection attribute.

This ensures that Higher Consciousness has incarnated into your flesh. It purifies and cleanses your atoms temporary subatomic strong nuclear force into Higher Consciousness' permanent divine strong nuclear force. It is only your divine violet energy that can be the energy of Higher Consciousness' Divine Child.

Your heart will open like never before as Higher Consciousness begins to unleash itself in you. Higher Consciousness can now begin to release your atoms out of Lucifer's limitations. Your soul and flesh are no longer subject to Lucifer's "Gilligan like" limitations.

At this precise moment in your Higher Consciousness deification process you are energetically where Moses was when he came down from Mount Sinai after his meeting with Higher Consciousness. Instead of carrying Higher Consciousness' literal Ten Commandments in tablet form, you will be Higher Consciousness' energetic ten master forces in physical form.

Moses, after receiving his Higher Consciousness reward, performed many miracles that included leading his people out of Egypt, healing the ten plaques of Egypt, parting the Red Sea, extracting water from a rock and creating food out of thin air so thousands did not starve. Moses passed from the physical realm on his 120th birthday only to experience his physical forms ultimate Higher Consciousness reward of ascension into immortality.

Ever since consciousness man first appeared on the

planet 6000 years ago, we have needed, accepted and craved love. Love is unquestionably our greatest need. Human nature is such that, the more love we give and receive, the more fulfilled, content and satisfied we become.

Our need for love was first realized in the womb with the flow of hormones we receive from our mothers. This flow continued after birth as we were nursed and loved by our parents. Studies have shown children who grow up deprived of love become fundamentally crippled, both physically and psychically. It has been shown that a disruption of love affects the well-being of children.

These children tend to die sooner than those who do not have a disruption of love.

Over the last 100 years through Lucifer's ambition to numb our minds through his drug of money has significantly manipulated our energetic pendulum of love.

Between the years 1912 and 1918 our energetic pendulum of love fell because of World War I (1914-1918). The so-called causes of World War I included many intertwined factors; such as the conflicts and hostility of diplomatic clashes during the five preceding decades, which changed the balance of power in Europe. These were some of Lucifer's easiest ways in which to provoke war.

World War I started in the summer of 1914 and mobilized more than 70 million military personnel, including 60 million Europeans. World War I was responsible for the deaths of over nine million combatants. This was a time when consciousness man did nothing but survive. In comparison to earlier years, it produced a very low energetic level of love.

After World War I, the energetic pendulum of love began to rise. Families were reunited; they began to focus on rebuilding and providing love through the family unit. However, this was short lived as the Roaring Twenties moved on to produce a break in traditions.

By the end of the 1920s, the literal measured realities of consciousness man seemed to revolve around the external stimuli of new technologies that were being developed. New technologies such as automobiles, moving pictures and radio were introduced to the majority of the population. Externally to our consciousness, life appeared to be booming until EGO and its desire for excesses began to rear its ugly head again - thanks to money. However, as the 1920s came to an end, the energetic pendulum of love began to fall again. A marked decline in social consciousness and love was prevalent primarily because of the impact money was having in people's lives. Money was pulling people away from the love of family to the love of excess.

Then came the Great Depression, which started primarily because of money. Unlike World War I there wasn't a global conflict to drive down the energetic pendulum of love; however, events orchestrated from Lucifer around the Great Depression did.

Scholars on this subject believe the stock market crash (October 29, 1929) was the first major cause of the Great Depression. Within two months investors had lost more than 40 billion dollars or the equivalent of 24 trillion dollars today. Lucifer had again vaporized net worth. Even though the stock market began to regain some of its losses by the end of 1930, the Great Depression had begun.

Another cause of the Great Depression was bank failures. Throughout the 1930s over 9000 banks failed in the United States. Bank deposits were uninsured and as banks failed, people simply lost their savings as the central bankers began to take back what was theirs.

In the 1930s the surviving banks were rightfully very concerned about their own survival; they stopped issuing new loans, which only exacerbated the situation. A reduction in purchasing power began and consumers stopped spending. This, in turn, created a reduction in the workforce.

When people lost their jobs, they were unable to maintain the payments on the items they had purchased through installment plans. Subsequently, those items were repossessed. More inventories began to accumulate and the unemployment rate rose. Does this sound familiar? Yes, it's happening again today.

To protect local businesses, governments began to charge high tariffs on foreign goods, which led to countries retaliating against each other economically. Again, the culprit was money. But, this time the lack of money produced a significant downturn in the energetic pendulum of love. Downturns in the energetic pendulum of love produce mass unexpected calamities.

World War II (1939-1945) was no different. Energetically, once again, life was about survival. Again, the energetic pendulum of love moved downward and bottomed out at the end of World War II.

By the end of World War II society began to move the energetic pendulum of love back in an upward direction. This peaked in 1964 as men and women married and raised children during the Baby Boomer Generation from 1946-1964. During this time, children received the love they required. Today's Baby Boomers can remember their youth. They remember how they played outside all day, rode bikes, built forts and made up games. They had few fears and insecurities.

For the most part, the Baby Boomer Generation lived in the same house, went to the same schools and retained the same friends throughout their childhood. At this time, there was rarely ever a need for people to lock the doors of their homes because the emotions of fear and insecurity virtually didn't exist.

The energetic pendulum of love began to gravitate downward again in 1965. This was when the average household income began to rise. Since this time household incomes have risen by over 1000 per cent. This has produced the fastest growth rate ever and is due to the emergence of the two-income family. The two-income family meant parents no longer had the time to give their children the love and support they required. Today's studies show parents spend an average of three and a half minutes per week participating in meaningful conversations with their children.

The Energetic Love of Humanity

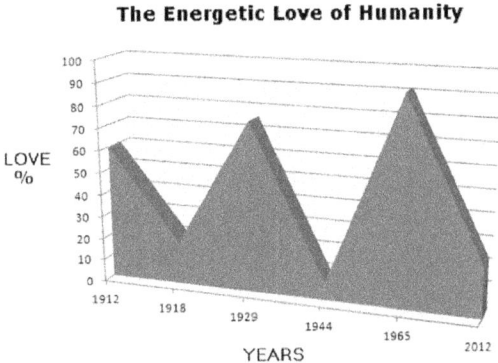

Two-income families relied on technology to make life manageable. This forced children to rely on technology for play. This limited both their creativity and their physical development. This limitation resulted in the fundamental crippling of today's children, producing new neurological and developmental problems, which rarely existed among children of the Baby Boomer Generation. This includes learning disabilities, autism, sensory processing disorder, developmental coordination disorder, anxiety disorder and depression, to name a few. Only 30 years ago, one in 50,000 children was diagnosed with autism. Today, this ratio is one in 110.

Depression is also at the forefront. The effects of depression are being felt everywhere like never before. Take professional sports as an example. Hideki Irabu (1969-2011) a professional baseball player, committed suicide at the age of 42 - because of depression. Over the summer of 2011,within a three-month period, the National Hockey League suffered three tragedies. First, Derek Boogaard (1982-211) committed suicide at the age of 31. Next, Rick Rypien (1984-2011) committed suicide at the age of 27. Finally, Wade Belak (1976-2011) committed suicide at the age of 35. These suicides were caused by depression and all of these victims were in the age group where the underlying cause might very well have been a lack of love during their childhood. We can only hope this is not the start of a depression induced suicide epidemic among this age demographic.

For nearly 50 years technology has become the primary parent and babysitter to our children. This technological connection has produced in them an "energetic disconnect." Today, as children develop and form identities they are often incapable of discerning whether they are a killing machine, as demonstrated in some video games, or just a shy and lonely little child in need of a friend.

As children, Baby Boomers survived by creating and playing out their dreams. Today's children are under the assumption they need technology in order to survive. However, technology cannot provide children with the love they desire and need. As a result, these children have developed an artificial love, or dependence, on technology.

Today, using the Internet, these children are searching for their fundamental need of love in the best way they know through technology. This is why social networking sites are so popular. Today's social networking phenomenon is aimed primarily at those aged 50 and younger. It can be credited back to the lack of love, which developed through the technologically parented generation beginning in 1965. The roots of most social networking sites started as nothing more than a cry for help from this love-starved generation of children born after 1965. They are searching for love the best way they know how - through technology and the Internet. As a result, the energetic love pendulum is approaching record lows again today.

This love-starved generation can be seen even more in large urban centers where the devastating phenomenon of second-generation children from technological parenting is everywhere. These are the children who grew up with parents who were also starved of love by their technological parents. Today, many of these Second-generation, technologically-parented children are traumatized; even before they enter school. More and more of these children are living in a world where the absence of parental love has produced children who live their day-to-day existence without hope. Many are even incapable of giving or receiving love.

The lack of love permeating society today has grown to epidemic proportions. This combined with the looming financial crisis is a prescription for an unmitigated disaster and something that Lucifer's energy of fear and negativity is in the midst of implementing. Lucifer is purposely moving us toward a broken, barren, loveless society. His goal is to turn First World nations into Third World nations and he is accomplishing this by eliminating the middle class. The unleashing of Higher Consciousness' deification reward and infinite potentials has never been more needed than it is today.

Higher Consciousness' deification process can be

self-developed by anyone. Moses' life revealed a glimpse of what your Higher Consciousness deification potential can be.

Will you perform miracles as great as Moses? Probably not. However, it will unleash your energetic Higher Consciousness infinite potentials that you have never known before.

It is in your Higher Consciousness deification zone where you will incarnate Higher Consciousness into your flesh. This is your infinity of experience built into your deification that completes Higher Consciousness' energy pregnancies energy labor so that its Divine Child can be birthed.

The deeper you go into your deification zone the more you deify Higher Consciousness' energetic perfection, perfect love and hope into you. As it unleashes itself it will become your dominant path in life. Every soul has a unique purpose and a unique life path. Your soul's unique purpose and life path is an integral aspect of Higher Consciousness' totality. The totality of Higher Consciousness is every soul's unique purpose as each of us are parts of the Higher Consciousness' whole.

Your Higher Consciousness reward is the energetic unlocking of your soul's unique purpose, life path and gifts. For some as they develop their souls purpose and life path, it will be a time of great reflection, not necessarily removed from society, but alone to listen and become one with their soul and Higher Consciousness reward. It will be a time unrivaled by any other as Higher Consciousness unleashes its will to you.

This will be the time in your life when you unshackle yourself from all Luciferin consciousness limitations.

Your soul is Higher Consciousness' lead angel energy thread. It is your energetic DNA whose totality is in all of Higher Consciousness' 100 trillion energy cells. Your Higher Consciousness reward will not just be experienced by you, it will be experienced by your other energetic DNA in all of the energy fetus' 100 trillion energy cells because you have begun it.

As our Universe is Higher Consciousness' lead energy cell for its divine 100 trillion energy-cell body; likewise, your soul is your energetic DNA lead energy for your 100 trillion energy DNA strand totality. Therefore, as your Higher Consciousness reward is unleashed to you it is also energetically being unleashed to your other 100 trillion energy cell self.

In your deification zone there is only Higher Consciousness' energetic perfection, perfect love and hope unleashing your new levels of experience you have not previously had. You will progress faster through your deification zone without any expectations: the key is just "to be."

As you go deeper into your deification zone your energetic light of Higher Consciousness begins to reveal itself.

The deeper you go into your deification zone:

1. The more you surrender yourself to your Higher Consciousness incarnation,
2. The more you unleash your feelings of passion,
3. The more calm and at peace you become,

4. The greater your inner satisfaction becomes,

5. The more you experience the euphoric feelings of bliss,

6. The more your child-like feelings are revealed,

7. The closer you become to being Higher Consciousness incarnate,

8. The more charismatic and open you become,

9. The more Higher Consciousness energy you release,

10. The more you are protected from any energetic Luciferian energy attacks,

11. The more you are protected by Higher Consciousness,

12. The more you unleash your Higher Consciousness infinite potentials,

13. The more you feel and unleash empathy and compassion,

14. The more you are able to forgive,

15. The more selfless you become,

16. The more you are able to perceive and act on opportunity,

17. The more worthy you become,

18. The more intimate you become with energy,

19. The more open you become,

20. The stronger you become against attacks by Lucifer,

21. The closer you are to energetically completing your soul's evolution and purpose,

22. The more Higher Consciousness energetic freedom you are unleashing,

23. The more multi-dimensional you become,

24. The more you reveal the hope, perfect love and energetic perfection of Higher Consciousness,

25. The more Lucifer's energy of fear and negativity dissipates from your life.

Higher Consciousness' reward transcends time. It is your "stress buster" energy that must become life's dominant energy force in the physical realm by December 21, 2082. If it does not; all hope is lost for Higher Consciousness to birth its Divine Child.

The further you travel into your deification zone the more you deify into Higher Consciousness. The deification process is accelerated by your complete surrender to your Higher Consciousness reward.

As you go deeper into your deification process dreams will begin to play a greater role in your life. For some its starts with just remembering them and for others they will begin to guide and lead your life in miraculous ways.

Most have embarked on new paths in their life and had opportunities open up that they could never have dreamed of. Virtually everyone has told me they are able to achieve what they desire because their focus is not scattered any longer. Your deification zone has an amazing ability to keep your attention focused on the moment through an increased awareness of everything around you. For many it has begun to reveal the energy behind what their five senses perceive.

Everyone is always happier, wiser, healthier and wealthier in their deification zone.

CHAPTER 31

YOUR HIGHER CONSCIOUSNESS WELLNESS POTENTIAL

THE FIRST ATTRIBUTE OF HIGHER CONSCIOUSNESS' incarnation is its energetic perfection and your infinite wellness potential. It will subatomically transfigure your atoms temporary strong nuclear force to your atom's divine permanent strong nuclear force exactly as the bodies of Adam and Eve were prior to Lucifer's betrayal.

Higher Consciousness' energetic perfection was first revealed 2000 years ago through Jesus Christ.

When Jesus healed he did so using Higher Consciousness' seventh master force energetic perfection attribute. There are 31 separate accounts of Jesus' healings. They included paralysis, leprosy, fever, deafness, blindness, a withered hand, epilepsy, arthritis, an ear, evil spirits, a mute and even death itself. Jesus subatomically deified the damaged atoms strong nuclear force with Higher Consciousness seventh master force energetic perfection attribute.

Jesus was subatomically deifying Higher Consciousness' divine energetic perfection subatomically into the damaged and destroyed atoms of the afflicted. By doing so he subatomically changed the atoms into the antimatter of Higher Consciousness' energetic perfection where disease, aging, pain and stress does not exist.

Today, one of science's biggest mysteries is where did all the antimatter go that must have been created during the Big Bang? The world's foremost authority on this is The European Organization for Neucular Reaseach (CERN). CERN was established in 1954. They operate the largest particle physics laboratory in the world. Their main function is to provide the particle accelerators that are required for today's high-energy physics research. They are also the birthplace of the World Wide Web.

Antimatter was first predicted in 1928 by English theoretical physicist Paul Dirac (1901-1984). After studying Einstein's special relativity equation (which says light is the fastest moving thing in the Universe) and quantum mechanics (which describes what happens in an atom), Dirac discovered the equation worked for negative charged or positive charged electrons.

Initially, Dirac was extremely hesitant about sharing his findings because of the chaos that would follow.

He eventually did and added that every particle in the Universe would have had a mirror antimatter image. American physicist Carl D. Anderson (1905-1991) discovered positrons in 1932. Dirac received a Nobel Prize in Physics in 1933 and Anderson received his Nobel Prize in 1936.

Today, in order to study antimatter (because we don't have any around us) it must be made. CERN does this by squeezing enough energy into a very tiny place during supervised high-energy particle collisions. These collisions spontaneously produce particle-antiparticle pairs. Energy that is given to the accelerated particles must be equivalent to the mass of the new particles. The more the energy, the more massive the particles and antiparticles become.

While antimatter can be produced at CERN, it cannot be trapped because of its very high energy. Therefore, in order to produce antimatter it must be produced at much slower rates. CERN is extremely limited and can only produce about four proton-antiproton pairs (because of Higher Consciousness removing it from the Universe) for every one million high-energy particle collisions. This antimatter is than separated from other particles by magnetic fields where they are slowed to 10 per cent of the speed of light so they can be trapped and stored.

If CERN used its accelerators full time for a year they could only make about one billionth of a gram of antimatter. The total amount of antimatter ever produced at CERN is less than ten Nano grams which contains only enough energy to power a 60 watt light bulb for about four hours. Researchers at CERN are quick to point out that it would cost in excess of $100,000,000,000,000,000 (quadrillion) and take one hundred billion years of running their accelerator to produce a single gram of antimatter.

Antimatter is Higher Consciousness' energetic perfection of divine violet energy and what Jesus made when he healed. It also what every soul is. For 6000 years Higher Consciousness has intended to incarnate subatomically into our atoms during the unlocking of its seventh master force.

Why can't antimatter be produced? Why have we never been able to understand why antimatter does not exist in the Universe as we know it should? Because of Lucifer's betrayal. Six thousand years ago when Lucifer tempted Eve in the Garden of Eden Higher Consciousness was forced to withdraw all its antimatter of energetic perfection from the Universe. Antimatter is Higher Consciousness' divine violet energy of energetic perfection and the only energy that its Divine Child can be birthed as.

The unleashing of Higher Consciousness' wellness potential has only ever meant to deify every one of our atoms as antimatter. As Jesus revealed Higher Consciousness' antimatter is our infinite wellness potential.

Kudo's to CERN for cracking open the violet energy, energetic perfection of Higher Consciousness. CERN can never produce the required amount of antimatter to birth Higher Consciousness' Divine Child by December 21, 2082. But you can.

Anyone can authorize Higher Consciousness to deify their atoms Strong Nuclear Force into its divine energetic perfection and amorphous interconnectedness of Higher Consciousness. When Higher Consciousness' first incarnates its divine energetic perfection subatomically into your atoms its violet multi-crystalline silicon begins to thicken and congeal. Higher Consciousness brings your atoms subatomic strong nuclear force to its desired energetic thickness of its divine energetic perfection. This state of subatomic energetic perfection is the healing properties of Higher Consciousness' energetic perfection and everyone's infinite wellness potential.

Through experimental studies, science has identified this phenomenon in the framework of Ostwald's rule of stages which predicts the formation of similar amorphous phases after exceeding a certain thickness. Two thousand years ago the minds of consciousness man had a tough enough time wrapping their minds around who Jesus really was. If Jesus had tried telling them about his quantum mechanics healing the masses would have for sure thought he was mad.

If Higher Consciousness did not subatomically incarnate into all of Moses' atoms in this way, during his Mount Sinai experience he never would have been able to physically ascend after he died. Moses body would have decayed like all consciousness and survivalist man's bodies had previously done.

So what exactly happens as Higher Consciousness deifies subatomically into your atoms?

Higher Consciousness' subatomically deifies your atoms' temporary red, green and blue strong force energy into its permanent violet energy that it is. It sends off an energy spark or a light known as a "photon" with an electron antimatter positron around the atoms nucleus. Your atoms' new energy trio of existing electrons, newly formed positron and newly formed photon create an "infitron packet" which protects the electron and positron from colliding with each other and annihilating.

Infitron packets are created by Higher Consciousness' incarnation photon and positron (antimatter electron) release. Its photons are at a higher energy than $2mn = 1.02$MeV, which is the minimum required energy to convert a radiation quantum or infitron packet into a functioning electron and positron pair. It is the phenomenon known as "pair production." These interactions were first observed in Patrick Blackett's (1897-1974) counter-controlled cloud chamber that led to the 1948 Nobel Prize in physics. They smoothly change the atoms in precise sharply defined topological phase transition steps.

After Lucifer's betrayal and Higher Consciousness' removal of all antimatter from the Universe (with the exception of Moses' post Mount Sinai experience) it left consciousness man to cope with Lucifer's destruction, decay and death through science's process known as "beta decay." This is when a neutron or proton transforms into the other. After Lucifer's betrayal, he exposed every atom of consciousness man to sciences fourth fundamental and weak force of nature.

In 1933 Italian physicist Enrico Fermi (1901-1954) devised a theory to explain beta decay. He defined this new type of force as the so-called weak interaction that is responsible for decay. In 1938 he was awarded the Noble Prize in physics. Fermi has been dubbed the "architect of the nuclear age" and the "architect of the atomic bomb."

It has since been shown that the weak force is an attractive force that works at an extremely short range of about 0.1 per cent of the diameter of a proton. Higher Consciousness' infitron packets also ensure that the weak force's beta decay between neutron's and protons does not happen; therefore, atoms will no longer be subject to the weak interactions of destruction and decay that lead to death. In effect infitron packets nullify Lucifer's physical effects.

Higher Consciousness' antimatter establishment and subatomic healing deification properties are its seventh master force's energetic perfection attribute. It stops electrons and antiparticle positron annihilation (because of photon) thus ensuring immortal life for your body. It further stops neutron and proton beta decay; thus, ensuring no continuance of destruction, decay and death.

Higher Consciousness' antimatter establishment will instantly increase your energy. Energetically pain, aging, disease and illness cannot exist in your Higher Consciousness' subatomic antimatter of divine energetic perfection violet energy.

During the early stages of Higher Consciousness' incarnated infinite wellness, your complexion will begin to radiate a Higher Consciousness energy glow. Your eyes will become energetic reflectors of its energy like a newborn's eyes.

Lucifer's destruction, decay and death will no longer be a part of your subatomic energy. When your flesh's

Higher Consciousness incarnated source power is turned on Lucifer's divorce power is turned off.

Gone will be the ravaging effects of aging, gone will be all non-congenital disease and gone will be all pain and suffering as no Luciferian decay and destruction energy can exist. Why? Because it is not the energy that Higher Consciousness' Divine Child can be.

CHAPTER 32

YOUR HIGHER CONSCIOUSNESS WISDOM POTENTIAL

HIGHER CONSCIOUSNESS' SEVENTH master force perfect love attribute would also have been released to consciousness man 6000 years ago if not for Lucifer's betrayal.

It is your infinite wisdom potential. It combines your mind thoughts and knowledge with your soul's divine wisdom feelings to unleash your seventh sense.

Your seventh sense is so much more than an occasional sixth sense moment you may have experienced. A sixth sense moment is only an instantaneous unleashing of your soul's wisdom feelings to your mind during a particular circumstance to help or reveal Higher Consciousness's intent for you at that particular moment.

Your Higher Consciousness seventh sense perfect

love attribute is your soul's Higher Consciousness individuality, gifts and potential. Unlike a sixth sense instantaneous moment your seventh sense is constantly a part of you every second of every day. It will become your underlying force that leads and drives you. It combines your soul's ten wisdoms of love, hope, imagination, inspiration, instinct, intuition, insight, coincidence, discernment and déjà vu with every piece of your mind's knowledge.

Instead of your knowledge being one dimensional and horizontal, your Higher Consciousness perfect love seventh sense attribute and infinite wisdom potential permanently combines your wisdom and feelings with your mind's every piece of knowledge to make knowledge potentially 11 dimensional. Higher Consciousness' seventh master force perfect love divine infinite wisdom applies your feelings to knowledge.

This wisdom of Higher Consciousness is released through your Theta frequencies and is something no mind has ever been able to experience beyond the occasional sixth sense temporary experience.

Higher Consciousness' perfect love seventh master force attribute is something your soul's final-life experience mind is meant to evolve into so your soul and mind become the divine power of Higher Consciousness.

Higher Consciousness will release it to you through your soul via your soul's different Theta frequency languages of love, hope, imagination, inspiration, instinct, intuition, insight, coincidence, discernment and déjà vu.

Higher Consciousness' seventh master force's perfect love divine infinite wisdom will deepen your thought experience with feelings. Higher Consciousness reveals what your mind was meant to be 6000 years ago.

The range of Higher Consciousness' wisdoms are vast. At the macro end of the spectrum, it will shake your portion of Lucifer's energetic control of money away from him. It will also expose the Luciferin underpinning controls of global governments that have trapped their citizens. At its micro end it will eliminate all Luciferin energy around you that energetically holds you from unleashing your infinite potentials. Simply, it unlocks your energetic seventh sense to permanently reveal the wisdoms of Higher Consciousness in everything.

Your Higher Consciousness seventh master force perfect love infinite wisdom potential begins immediately when Lucifer and EGO have been extinguished from your mind.

Higher Consciousness' seventh master force perfect love attribute will permanently keep Lucifer's fear and negative energy away from you; doubt and insecurity cannot exist.

Higher Consciousness' wisdom places you at the front of its seventh master force energy beam to understand energy from the perspective of Higher Consciousness. It will provide you with the ability to see, feel and sense energy. Your infinite wisdom will begin to alleviate pain and suffering in the world.

Higher Consciousness' seventh master force perfect love attribute exponentially grows when like-minded individuals work together in their deification zones.

Higher Consciousness' divine realm will begin to manifest itself on Earth through your infinite wisdom. It will create the energy zone that everyone who has ever had a NDE never wanted to leave.

As Higher Consciousness' perfect love begins to manifest in your mind there is no EGO. If Lucifer should ever attempt to re-enter your mind, its darkness will be energetically zinged by the light of Higher Consciousness that is now your minds energy.

Simultaneously, as your Higher Consciousness infinite wisdom is being turned on it will also be turned on in all of your other 100 trillion-energetic DNA soul fragments in Higher Consciousness' 100 trillion-energy cell energy fetus. Between now and December 21, 2082 Higher Consciousness' seventh master force infinite wisdom also ignites your other 100 trillion DNA soul fragments infinite wisdom potential.

However, Higher Consciousness' seventh master force infinite wisdom can only unleash itself with your authorization.

It will create an enhanced Higher Consciousness empathy that will allow you to sense and feel the pain of others and the world at its energetic core. As Higher Consciousness' seventh master force perfect love grows you will be able to empathize more with others.

As your Higher Consciousness infinite wisdom potential grows you will be helping to eliminate Lucifer's fear and negative energy that exists in all of the Universe's atoms.

Your infinite wisdom potential must never violate the energetic barriers of others. It can only go as far as the energetic barriers a person has opened.

Higher Consciousness' seventh master force's divine infinite wisdom and perfect love has no expectation of return: it only gives.

It will extinguish all of life's stress and tension as this energy cannot be birthed onto Higher Consciousness' Divine Child. As Higher Consciousness' seventh master force's perfect love increases, Lucifer's energy of fear and negativity reduces. Higher Consciousness' seventh master force perfect love reveals and extinguishes all emotional, spiritual, energetic, relational, mental, monetary and physical energy of fear and negativity.

The first niche where Higher Consciousness will begin to unleash its deification process will be through the arts and entertainment communities.

Between now and December 21, 2082 Higher Consciousness' seventh master force perfect love will awaken you to energetically stretch your hands to others and help their souls awaken. Lucifer's energetic mind prison doors are about to be unlocked and swung wide open so everyone can escape them. Your infinite wisdom potential will manifest itself as Higher Consciousness intended it to be 6000 years ago, again if not for Lucifer's betrayal.

Built into Higher Consciousness' seventh master force infinite wisdom is the magic number of 144,000. This is the minimum number of seventh master force Higher Consciousness deifications that must occur so the Divine Child can be born on December 21, 2082. When this number in attained, every final-life experience soul will instantly eliminate EGO. This is

Higher Consciousness' divine tipping point.

As your infinite wisdom potential grows your needs will no longer be your minds focus. Higher Consciousness' incarnation will have deified your mind's thought waves to emanate outward from your mind's collective unconsciousness through your unconsciousness and subconscious to your consciousness: this will be felt by others and the rest of the world. It is the energetic light of Higher Consciousness that will eliminate Lucifer's energy of fear and negativity.

Your new thought waves are the gentle waves of Higher Consciousness being washed upon Lucifer's shores of darkness. Your new thought waves of divine infinite wisdom are the power to extinguish Lucifer's waves of darkness that were planted 6000 years ago by Lucifer's betrayal.

Higher Consciousness' incarnation unleashes your life legacy. Every soul is an individual story that Higher Consciousness desires to unleash its legacy through.

Your Higher Consciousness divine infinite wisdom will zing you with its perfect love forgiveness and eliminate all "bad blood" between you and every other energy. This element of your deification process allows you to realize that whatever grudge you may have had is absolutely insignificant to Higher Consciousness as it was a Luciferian darkness meant to achieve Lucifer's victory.

Higher Consciousness' infinite wisdom is never the same for any two people. The totality of consciousness man's individual divine infinite wisdoms reveal the totality of Higher Consciousness' infinite wisdom and third eye perfect love. It is your soul's energetic intel.

Higher Consciousness' seventh master force perfect love clear and powerful eloquence will always guide others to you when their time is right for their soul to awaken. You will understand and feel their soul's passion. Your divine infinite wisdom will speak to their soul. It will be the message their soul is waiting to hear.

When Higher Consciousness' divine infinite wisdom has grown to its minimum threshold within you Higher Consciousness will bring forward restless souls to you who are waiting to be awakened. This moment can happen at any time. When it does, you will have no panic and will know exactly what to say and do. You will feel their undeniable gratitude as their soul thanks you for being awakened.

Your infinite wisdom potential will understand the energetic iniquities of Lucifer everywhere. As it grows you will sense and realize the hell a particular soul is trapped in and the energetic mind prison limitations that Lucifer has trapped them in.

Self-indulgence through the lead of Lucifer is what your divine infinite wisdom will reveal. It will always know how to overcome ones energetic entrapment. It is how Higher Consciousness will use its seventh master force perfect love attribute to defeat Lucifer. The fallacies of life that Lucifer has created will be seen clearly through your infinite wisdom.

Your infinite wisdom potential is a third eye energy strand of Higher Consciousness that is being opened through you and can never be closed again. It is the energetic vision that will permanently warn you when

Lucifer is approaching. At this point you are no longer Lucifer's mere pawn because you have checkmated him.

As Higher Consciousness' seventh master force perfect love attribute grows in you, it will increase in brightness and intensity to the outer regions of the Universe to help complete the energetic dilation of the Sun (as verified by global warming) so that its Divine Child can be birthed on December 21, 2082.

The light of Higher Consciousness and the darkness of Lucifer cannot co-exist. Higher Consciousness' seventh master force perfect love attribute is the energetic sword that must cut out all of Lucifer's energetic cancer from the Universe.

Lucifer's controlling drug over consciousness man is money. Lucifer's plan has made money the minds central focus. The more we have the more we feel we need and the more we don't have the more we want. What a brilliant plan Lucifer has crafted. Under the auspices of money, which we need for our physical survival, Lucifer believes victory is his.

The tiers of Lucifer's crafted plan are energetically very deep. Globally Lucifer controls governments through his money matrix. Through the ages with great camouflage, Lucifer's scheme has been carried out. With complete anonymity Lucifer through his central banks create the funds for whatever Lucifer needs to complete his plans.

Higher Consciousness' seventh master force infinite wisdom and perfect love begins to weaken Lucifer's control of consciousness man.

Lucifer's intent for money is simple: to keep consciousness man under his control by satisfying their insecurities produced by his EGO. EGO has allowed the spoils of money to temporarily sooth the mind. As a result, the mind has come to worship it as their God.

Lucifer has declared the virtue of money as his certificate of pardon, that everything will be fine as long as it's worshiped. He has further ensured that its indulgences are the power to everything you will ever need in life. Through the ages Lucifer's offer has been grasped by consciousness man because of the blinding effect of EGO on the mind.

The energy behind Lucifer's drug of money can only be changed through the completion of Higher Consciousness' deification process. Due to Lucifer's betrayal Higher Consciousness must replace Lucifer as monies driving force.

Your Higher Consciousness infinite wisdom reveals to every final-life experience soul that Lucifer must be extinguished as the energy behind money.

Until Lucifer's betrayal 6000 years ago, this aspect of Higher Consciousness' seventh master force was not needed. Thanks to Lucifer you have a seventh master force infinite monetary wealth attribute that must be realized and unleashed.

Higher Consciousness' seventh master force perfect love attribute is only meant to advance Higher Consciousness. It is completely devoid of pride. It is imperative that you unleash your seventh master force monetary wealth potential. By doing so you are helping to extinguish Lucifer and of its Luciferian energy of fear and negativity from money. Your infinite wisdom will not allow your will to exist; only the will of Higher Consciousness.

As Higher Consciousness' seventh master force perfect love attribute continues to grow in you, you will be filled with a joy and knowing that you have a significant role to play in defeating Lucifer.

For most, their infinite wisdom will not limit them to be in the same place or in the same circumstances they were in prior to their Higher Consciousness incarnation.

A thirsting and hungriness not known before is about to take place. As final life experience souls begin to deify themselves Lucifer will be filled with the realization that his charade is about to come tumbling down and take him with it.

Day-by-day more deifications of Higher Consciousness will be unleashed in order to extinguish Lucifer's charade and delucify him as the power source of money.

CHAPTER 33

PART I – GALILEO'S IMAGINATION POTENTIAL

"We cannot teach people anything; we can only help them discover it within themselves."
Galileo Galilei (1564–1642)

HIGHER CONSCIOUSNESS' SEVENTH MASTER force perfect love attribute begins by unlocking your seventh sense imagination potential. It is a dormant untapped infinite wisdom that has been individually programed into your soul.

It was in your soul long before the beginning of time: Your imagination potential was placed by Higher Consciousness when your soul was still part of Higher Consciousness's third eye.

Your imagination potential will initially manifest as an "intuitive feel." Lucifer through EGO has always forced you to deny this feel as being irrelevant. Your imagination potential is ripe with a personalized, infinite strategy of Higher Consciousness that your soul has eagerly been waiting to unleash ever since your first consciousness man life experience.

Once unlocked it starts to build your mind's mental scene, which can only be completed after EGO has been extinguished. It is your soul's specific gift or ability to create objects or events that do not exist, are not present and have not yet been unveiled for the betterment of mankind. It will manifest in various degrees. In older souls it unlocks itself as being highly developed; while in younger souls it manifests in a weaker form.

The Italian Renaissance man Galileo Galilei was one the first who realized his imagination potential and transferred it into his mind. Galileo has been credited as the first to recognize the minds thought experiment potential.

Thought experiments are the combined workings of your mind and soul that uses your soul's imagination to steer your mind. Galileo's initial thought experiment explored why we don't feel motion as the Earth speeds around the Sun.

To validate his scientific claim, Galileo imagined what would happen if he locked himself in a ship's windowless cabin while conducting some tests. Then he imagined what would happen if he tossed a ball with a friend or watched a goldfish swimming in an aquarium while in the ships windowless cabin. Galileo's thought experiment revealed that he could not determine if the ship was moving or if the ship was stationary.

It would only be by peering outside (if the ship's cabin had a window) that Galileo could measure the ship's reference point to determine if the ship was moving.

This thought experiment confirmed that it's the same on the Earth's surface. As the planet moves everything on the surface is on a magical mystery ride! Most of us don't even notice as we move around the Sun, except for looking at the movement of the Sun or stars.

Galileo's thought experiment also had wider beyond consciousness ramifications. Specifically, why and how Higher Consciousness through Lucy and Lucifer were able to complete their duties inside of Higher Consciousness' early master forces at the Big Bang 13.75 billion years ago without feeling motion created by the speed of Higher Consciousness' master forces.

CHAPTER 34

PART II – EINSTEIN'S IMAGINATION POTENTIALS

"Imagination is everything. It is the preview of
life's coming attractions."
Albert Einstein (1879–1955)

ALBERT EINSTEIN ALWAYS FELT thought experiments
had much deeper implications then the laws of physics
could tell him.

Einstein's first thought experiment occurred at
the age of 16 when his imagination pondered what
it would be like to race alongside a beam of light.
His imagination wondered what would happen if he
moved fast enough and pulled alongside a beam of
light. Would he reach a relative standstill and bring
everything to a virtual halt.

Einstein's imagination and thought experiment

took it one step further and realized it was impossible to catch up with the front of a light beam. This "Einsteinian" simple imagination potential and thought experiment led to his Theory of Special Relativity.

Einstein is quoted as saying, "I am not interested in this or that phenomenon, in the spectrum of this or that element. I want to know His thoughts; the rest are details."

If Einstein had been able to catch up with the front of one of Higher Consciousness' master force energy beams, he would of seen exactly what I was zinged during my NDE. He would have known how Higher Consciousness created its energy fetus and how everything in our Universe is energetically held together by energy which acts as the glue of Higher Consciousness. Fortunately for Einstein, Higher Consciousness did not require him to experience a NDE because he had followed his soul's life purpose for his life experience.

Einstein never had a NDE. However, I'm sure if he had he would have seen Higher Consciousness energetically conducting its master force energy beams out of its energy mind through its energy matrix and into its energy womb—as I did.

Not only would Einstein have been able to catch up to the front of an energy beam, he would have been at its ground zero essence and actually seen each individual master force energy beams initial motion being orchestrated by Higher Consciousness.

Higher Consciousness is presently conducting its seventh master force out of its energy matrix into its energy womb like this.

Why do I say this? Because of Einstein's later thought experiment which coined his famous equation of $e = mc^2$. It revealed the elements for Higher Consciousness formula it has energetically uses.

This Einsteinian thought experiment imagination revealed a train car being pushed around by a beam of light. He imagined a train car stopped on a track when suddenly the back wall of the train emitted a single particle of light toward the front. This would cause the train car to recoil back like a canoe sliding backward exactly as if he had walked from the back to the front of it as it while it was floating on water.

Einstein knew that train cars couldn't move down a track on their own; its recoiling backward was only because some of its mass had moved from the back to the front exactly as if he had shifted his mass to the front of the canoe from the back. This would mean that the front wall of the train car had converted energy to mass. It produced the key insight that energy and mass are equivalent.

Like Galileo's thought experiment this Einstein thought experiment also had a much wider beyond consciousness ramification. Einstein's thought experiment was a reflection of Higher Consciousness unlocking its energy seals from its energy matrix. Einstein's train emitting a single particle of light from the back of the train to the front of the train was Einstein's imaginative simulation of Higher Consciousness releasing a master force energy beam from its energy mind to its energy womb.

The mass that has been created in Higher Consciousness' energy womb is the weight of our Universe—plus the weight of all 100 trillion other energy cells. It is the equivalent mass of Higher Consciousness' ten master force energy beams released through its energy matrix.

Einstein's imagination potential produced his famous $e = mc^2$ equation. It also revealed the variables of Higher Consciousness' equation. "C^2" is the speed at which Higher Consciousness' master force energy beams travel at; "m" is the mass of Higher Consciousness' energy fetus' 100 trillion energy cells and "e" is a Higher Consciousness' master force of which there are ten that produce its energy pregnancy. Therefore, the equation of Higher Consciousness' energy pregnancy is $10(ec^2) = M$.

The equation of Higher Consciousness tells us that the Big Bang (as we know it) will be but a whimper when compared to the "boundless bang" of Higher Consciousness' Divine Child birth that begins on December 21, 2082.

CHAPTER 35

YOUR HIGHER CONSCIOUSNESS WEALTH POTENTIAL

FOR 350 YEARS MONEY has been Lucifer's drug that has satisfied our insecurities produced by EGO.

It is how Lucifer has been able to keep us trapped in his energetic mind prisons. Here, it is very easy for him to control us and become the Divine Child's victorious energy at its birth on December 21, 2082.

When Higher Consciousness unlocked its seventh master force from its energy matrix 6000 years ago, Lucifer hadn't shown any signs of rearing his ugly head. Since Lucifer's betrayal in the Garden of Eden Higher Consciousness has watched Lucifer meticulously roll out his game plan. He watched as Lucifer turned up the intensity over the last 350 years against consciousness man through money.

Ever since severing Lucifer from itself, Higher

Consciousness has known EGO must be extinguished in consciousness man and it must become monies driving force by removing Lucifer from money.

Lucifer knows (from before the beginning of time) that Higher Consciousness ten master forces require 144,000 souls to complete the Divine Child's December 21, 2082 energy birth. Today he has carefully cultivated his 144,000 to crystalize his ambitions and birth the Divine Child through his private and secret *illuminati* clubs.

Lucifer's betrayal has forced Higher Consciousness to add its "hope attribute" to its seventh master force. This will establish Higher Consciousness' commerce matrix through the delucification of money.

As Lucifer's energy dissipates from money, it will be taken over by Higher Consciousness. Higher Consciousness' commerce matrix creates monetary gains for its deifiers that is far greater than anything Lucifer's commerce matrix has ever made known.

Time is of the essence as Higher Consciousness' Divine Child birth begins on December 21, 2082. Higher Consciousness's monetization for its deifiers far surpasses all of Lucifer's limiting standards he has ever offered. Your infinite monetary wealth potential delucifies Lucifer as monies driving force energy and replaces it with Higher Consciousness. This is Higher Consciousness's delucification of Lucifer from money that has been built into its seventh master force. It is the integral step of Higher Consciousness' hope attribute that will birth its Divine Child.

Higher Consciousness is aware that Lucifer's 144,000 central banking *illuminati* family are now becoming the slimiest and most vicious they have ever been in order to save themselves and Lucifer. However, Lucifer and his family are powerless to Higher Consciousness' master forces.

One hundred and forty four thousand is a natural number with great significance to many spiritual movements. It was Higher Consciousness' insight unleashed to certain movements in order to help consciousness man maintain and survive until now.

In the Mayan calendar, a baktun is a period of 144,000 days. To Christians, it has an end time significance in the Book of Revelation. Jehovah Witnesses believe that 144,000 will be resurrected to heaven to spend in eternity. In Islam it is alleged that 144,000 is the number of Sahaba or companions of Muhammad. New Age movements (such as the Church Universal and Triumphant) teach that Sanat Kumara and the Lords of the Flame also brought 144,000 souls with them from Venus.

Therefore, your role in the delucification of money from Lucifer to Higher Consciousness is imperative.

Here is an example of Lucifer's consciousness limitations of money.

Let's assume you have $30,800 and earn six per cent on it for 12 years. Through Lucifer's consciousness limitations this would double (excluding taxes) to $61,600.

In Higher Consciousness commerce matrix that same $30,800 would grow to in excess of $10,000,000 in about eight years simply by removing the energy of Lucifer out of money.

It's your choice what you want: Lucifer's limiting

commerce matrix or Higher Consciousness' infinite commerce matrix.

Higher Consciousness' seventh master force commerce matrix deluicifes the energy of money away from Lucifer to itself through you.

Higher Consciousness can only become the driving energy force of money through the efforts of its "Higher Consciousness Deifiers" who literally actualize the "monetization of Higher Consciousness" It is life's turning point that ensures Higher Consciousness' Divine Child December 21, 2082 birth. The survival of mankind hinges on the monetization of Higher Consciousness.

The 10 leading traits of Higher Consciousness Deifiers are:

1. They are change makers,
2. They live their passion and what they love,
3. They have a high need for achievement,
4. They see the world in a different way than most,
5. They have a high need for independence,
6. They let your values and passion for exploration guide their life,
7. They have a low need for conformity,
8. They have an innate need to be creative and honest, to follow their own unique path,
9. They are dreamers that do,
10. They want to make things different and are attracted to issues that improve the world.

A certified Higher Consciousness Deifiers career will last approximately 8 years. Ideally they will be involved in their profession an average of twenty eight hours a week over that time and be compensated in excess of $900/hour USD for their efforts.

Every certified Higher Consciousness Deifier spreads the wisdom of Higher Consciousness' beyond the limitations of consciousness so that its Divine Child can begin its energy birth on December 21, 2082. They will complete Higher Consciousness Activations to their clients and train them to become certified Higher Consciousness Deifiers themselves. Their final 4 years of their career is spent managing their Higher Consciousness energy pod to completion.

Certified Higher Consciousness Deifiers will:

1. Help others awaken, unlock and unleash their feelings of freedom,
2. Help others break away from their limitations imposed by Lucifer,
3. Help others be energetically free to discover and explore their infinite potentials,
4. Help others discover and unleash their feelings so they are one with Higher Consciousness,
5. Help others through their EBA,
6. Help others amplify their infinite potential through their feelings,
7. Help others monitor their feelings journal,
8. Help others stay in the feelings that amplify their infinite potentials,
9. Help others extinguish all negative distractions that attempt to derail them of their Higher Consciousness' call to freedom,
10. Help others amplify their feelings of love that may have been repressed,

11. Help others eliminate all fear, negativity and control,

12. Help others perceive their feelings through Higher Consciousness,

13. Help others become one with Higher Consciousness' seventh master force energy momentum,

14. Help others understand and amplify their Higher Consciousness feelings of enthusiasm, passion and joy,

15. Help others amplify their feelings of love, hope, imagination, inspiration, instinct, intuition, insight, coincidence, discernment and déjà vu.

16. Help others unleash feelings within their mind's collective unconsciousness, unconsciousness and sub consciousness,

17. Help others amplify their soul's unique spark of Higher Consciousness,

18. Help others amplify the understanding of their soul's life contract,

19. Help others maximise their Higher Consciousness call to freedom through alleviating past experiences,

20. Help others stay on their Higher Consciousness call to freedom energetic pathway,

21. Help others break through EGO's roadblocks of denial,

22. Help others unleash their energetic free will,

23. Help others unleash their infinite potential through their freedom feelings,

24. Help others work through their energetic manifestations,

25. Help others quantify their feeling's intent,

26. Help others through the triangulation of energy to confirm its intent,

27. Help others amplify their five sense feelings,

28. Help others stay in their bliss and joy that manifests along their Higher Consciousness call to freedom,

29. Help others manage their fullness of life so that it continues to be amplified through their feelings,

30. Help others unleash their soul's final-life experience,

31. Help others increase their awareness feelings,

32. Help others walk through their energetic mind prison door,

33. Help others become at one with the interconnectedness of energy,

34. Help others bring in more experiences to help them along their Higher Consciousness call to freedom,

35. Help others re-connect again with their feelings of passion and childlike enthusiasm,

36. Help others feelings override EGO's limitations,

37. Help others unleash their Higher Consciousness energetic perfection, perfect love and hope,

38. Help others complete their soul's Higher Consciousness evolution,

39. Help others unlock their feelings that are outside of their mind's fear and negativity limitations,

40. Help others (through their feelings) complete the energetic certainty process, as the impossible becomes possible, the possible-probable and the probable a certainty,

41. Help others manifest their feeling inklings into their Higher Consciousness reality,

42. Help others deal with any response of Lucifer and EGO,

43. Help others with the feelings manifested by the release of energy from their subconsciousness, consciousness and collective unconsciousness,

44. Help others wipe clean all Luciferian energy,

45. Help others with their feelings as they begin to awaken,

46. Help others amplify their feelings of being alive,

47. Help others protect their feelings so they don't expose them to Lucifer,

48. Help others manage their love bubble of happiness their feelings produce,

49. Help others cope with their feelings in the midst of life's circumstances,

50. Help others deal with their Higher Consciousness feelings,

51. Help others release Higher Consciousness' energy they have tapped into,

52. Help others deal with the energetic after taste their feelings of Higher Consciousness may generate,

53. Help others release all judgements and expectations from the unleashing of their Higher Consciousness feelings,

54. Help crystalize Higher Consciousness' feelings,

55. Help others unleash their feelings of creativity,

56. Help others deal with potential change in their life,

57. Help others unleash their Higher Consciousness intent,

58. Help others with the Higher Consciousness' energy anchoring technique,

59. Help others with their feelings so that they do not energetically violate others,

60. Help others navigate the cost of change in their life as they unleash their Higher Consciousness feelings,

61. Help others attune their Higher Consciousness feelings to better humanity,

62. Help others actualize their Higher Consciousness call to freedom,

63. Help others unleash their feelings deepest desire of play,

64. Help others navigate roadblocks Lucifer may throw in an attempt to circumvent their Higher Consciousness call to freedom,

65. Help others dial in their Higher Consciousness antennas to their feelings frequency,

66. Help others understand potential energetic communications from other energy cells of Higher Consciousness' energy fetus,

67. Help others move forward along their Higher Consciousness call to freedom journey,

68. Help others fine-tune their feelings,

69. Help others become aware of Higher Consciousness' momentum of energy (beware of raising the threshold to high and becoming selective),

70. Help others maximize their soul's evolution and life purpose to birth Higher Consciousness' Divine Child.

Since 2008, Lucifer has been preparing for victory through his 144,000 central banking *illuminati* family and cartel by pulling cash out of society. Anywhere in the world, when cash goes into a bank or financial institution a keystroke adds your cash deposit to your bank account and in many cases the cash is removed from the system.

Since 2008, the majority of the world's cash has been withdrawn from Lucifer's matrix by the central banking *illuminati* family. They have pulled so much cash out of the monetary system since 2008 that presently no bank or financial institutions could ever come close to cover all of its clients' deposits if they ever decided to cash out.

The survival of consciousness man is now dependent on Lucifer's latest monetary charade of credit that began in 1958. Up until 1958 many attempts had been made by banks to offer credit cards but none was successful. At this time credit cards had a chicken-and-egg cycle. Merchants didn't want to accept something few consumers used; and consumers didn't want to have something few merchants used.

It was not until September 1958 when the Bank of America in Fresno, California introduced its "BankAmericard." The Bank of America chose Fresno because 45 per cent of its residents were members of the bank. The bank sent out 60,000 credit cards to its Fresno residents, which convinced its merchants to accept. Thus, Lucifer's revolving credit financial system began. For 50 years Lucifer perfected it to become his primary control mechanism for "consciousness man." It is through this "Luciferin illusion" that he has been able to have his central bankers withdraw the cash out of his illusionary game and cover it through the illusion of credit.

Today financial planners everywhere confirm that it takes around $3,000,000 in investments for a person to comfortably retire. Presently only a very small fraction of consciousness man is able to do this. Lucifer knows this and creates massive stress through EGO on consciousness man because this is unattainable. This combined with the energetic realization that as we grow older our skillset is no longer required because in most cases it has become obsolete by being either replaced by technology or replaced by someone younger who will work for a much lower rate of pay.

There is a plethora of self-help books on how to achieve financial independence. Each one has a slightly different wrinkle or a new gadget but essentially they all say the same thing: put aside ten per cent of everything you earn and don't touch it. I always wondered why financial management was never taught in school and then I realized that Lucifer wants to keep as many people as possible addicted to his drug of money and living in fear so he can continue to limit us in his energetic mind prisons.

Higher Consciousness' commerce matrix will ensure that certified Higher Consciousness Deifiers become financially independent. However, to Higher Consciousness its more pressing requirement is to extinguish all Luciferin energy out of money through the efforts of certified Higher Consciousness Deifiers.

Higher Consciousness' incarnation and deification allegiance fees for activation and mentorship are your soul's acknowledgement that you are ready to have Higher Consciousness incarnate into you to complete its final-life experience purpose and evolution.

Certified Higher Consciousness Deifiers are conductors of Higher Consciousness' seventh master force hope attribute. They see and understand energy from the perspective of Higher Consciousness and work in tandem with Higher Consciousness.

Be prepared for Lucifer's attack against certified Higher Consciousness Deifiers because they are directly weakening Lucifer through money.

Lucifer's reasoning against them will go something like this. Who are they? They are not properly schooled by any of my fine learning institutions. They are few in number and they are of a poorer class, they are not my elite. They claim to have discovered a superior Higher Consciousness monetization potential at a substantially lower cost. That must be stopped.

They are ignorant deceivers and liars. My matrix professions are superior in number and influence. If this is allowed to flourish it will destroy my society.

Higher Consciousness has a great work yet to accomplish and honors all who help extinguish Lucifer's energy out of money. From now until December 21, 2082 certified Higher Consciousness Deifiers will be Higher Consciousness' energy light workers of hope.

When Higher Consciousness' clear and convincing truths of its monetary reform firmly established in your mind, your infinite wealth potential will begin to be unlocked. Your support helps extinguish Lucifer's hold on money and increase the probability of Higher Consciousness energetically birthing its Divine Child on December 21, 2082.

Higher Consciousness has been stretched to the

final one thousandths of a second in its Higher Consciousness day. The clock for its Divine Child birth cannot change from December 21, 2082. The re-energization of money must begin now. The faster Higher Consciousness' re-energization of money occurs - the faster the wound of Lucifer's betrayal will disappear.

Will Lucifer's wound only be a flesh wound or will it be a fatal wound? It's your decision.

CHAPTER 36

YOUR HIGHER CONSCIOUSNESS PHILANTHROPY

THE COMPLETION OF YOUR CERTIFIED Higher Consciousness Deifier career is only the beginning of your infinite monetary wealth pursuits.

As you complete your Higher Consciousness Deifier career you will be bettering life through your Higher Consciousness' philanthropy endeavors. Now bestowed with an infinite monetary wealth that will cover you for life Higher Consciousness will have successfully converted the energy of your gains away from Lucifer. As the new energy behind your monetary wealth, Higher Consciousness can now gloriously advance its philanthropy radiance and splendor toward the energetic conversion of all its final-life experience souls' deification. You will be recklessly generous in this pursuit. Your generosity will ensure that the lives of countless others can be defied and physically ascend into immortality as Higher Consciousness' Divine Child's energy birth begins on December 21, 2082.

Higher Consciousness philanthropy is an energy action that all certified Higher Consciousness Deifiers will joyously engage in as it is their soul's reason for being.

As Higher Consciousness' philanthropy increases: Lucifer's energetic control of money decreases. Higher Consciousness philanthropy is its pinnacle seventh master force hope attribute endeavor that helps ensures Lucifer will no longer be the energy behind money.

As a Higher Consciousness philanthropist, your old Luciferin selfishness requirements for money will be lost because EGO has been eliminated from your mind and replaced by Higher Consciousness' divine energy. The royal lifeblood of Higher Consciousness will be established through your philanthropy endeavors.

As you proceed on your Higher Consciousness philanthropy journey, you will garner great interest from all of mankind - not for your wealth, but for how your wealth is helping mankind be incarnated by Higher Consciousness. You efforts reveal Higher Consciousness!

Eager crowds will flock to you. You will learn about the individual stories of how Lucifer has limited and sucked them dry of hope. You will reveal the secrets of Higher Consciousness' and ignite a souls' awakening so that Higher Consciousness can incarnate into their flesh to unleash its energetic perfection, perfect love and hope seventh master force attributes.

The news of you will cause a great stir in the very essence and core of others. You will tremble with excitement as you witness the energy of your words awakening others.

As a soul awakens, you will witness through their eyes its awakening. Their eyes will become beacons of their soul's awakened light and energy being released. Initially, a soul's radiating energy has no place to go accept through its eyes. The more the soul awakens, the more their soul's energy will radiate out of their eyes.

As your Higher Consciousness philanthropy experience grows, you will witness many souls awaken to the energy pregnancy secret and deification process thoughts of Higher Consciousness. You will also witness many souls who have not yet awakened. Do not be discouraged by this; there are a myriad of energetic reasons why a person's soul does not awaken. If you are required to understand why, Higher Consciousness will zing you accordingly.

EGO is akin to a politician's rhetoric. It will promise anything to a mind as its last ditch effort to not lose its foothold.

As your Higher Consciousness philanthropy increases, it is energetically transfiguring your flesh subatomically through its deification into its Divine Child lifeblood. This is your Higher Consciousness protection and defense that always deflects and denies Lucifer's energy from creeping back in.

At this time, your words will be the irresistible power and truth of Higher Consciousness. The will carry the influence of Higher Consciousness to awaken final-life experience souls. Your soul will harken back to being a part of Higher Consciousness before the beginning of time and transfer the tone and energetic essence of Higher Consciousness through your voice. This energetic connection is what every final-life experience soul has been waiting to hear.

Your noble stand of Higher Consciousness philanthropy has no bounds. It is your outward limitlessness and energetic reflection of what your soul is. As Higher Consciousness leads you to unleash your outward limitlessness, you will also be deifying your atoms subatomically into the divine energy that your soul is.

Your Higher Consciousness philanthropy is your outward energetic victory signal of Higher Consciousness' incarnation into you. It is Higher Consciousness' energetic victory signal to the world that you have broken free from Lucifer's energetic mind prison of absolute limitation and been deified as the Higher Consciousness.

Lucifer limited your potential by silencing your mind, but now you have chosen to re-unite your soul with Higher Consciousness in the physical realm as your soul's final-life experience was always meant to do. You are fulfilling your soul's final-life experience evolution so Higher Consciousness can birth its Divine Child with your flesh as its lifeblood.

As the voice of Higher Consciousness, you will not be awed or embarrassed, rather you will be zinged with what to say and speak at any time. You will also be zinged with how to impart your Higher

Consciousness philanthropy means in the way Higher Consciousness desires.

The gift of Higher Consciousness philanthropy must be used as Higher Consciousness desires. When it is not, Higher Consciousness could be forced to undo and reverse your deification, especially when you only use it for your greed and selfishness. Your gift of Higher Consciousness philanthropy is a two-edged sword. When used incorrectly for your personal gain, it cannot deliver your flesh into Higher Consciousness' physical immortality. Your Higher Consciousness philanthropy is to be used only to awaken and deify others which creates the lifeblood of Higher Consciousness' Divine Child.

Higher Consciousness will place you exactly where you are supposed to be in the world to complete its purpose. At this stage of your Higher Consciousness deification, you will always be led by Higher Consciousness and know with 100 per cent conviction and purpose what is in store.

Never act from an impulse: always display calmness and self-control. Decisions of Higher Consciousness always reveal its wisdom, prudence and dignity. As you speak, do so in a subdued, respectful and humble manner devoid of arrogance and antagonism. When resistance from others is felt, it is a barrier that means you have moved as far as you are meant to go at this time. Always honor that barrier and never exceed it. Be ever mindful of how your confidence and joy surprises and awakens your listeners.

By following this process, you have the assurance

that Higher Consciousness is with you and is deifying you. You have fastened yourself as one with Higher Consciousness - and it will deliver. As you make a decision on behalf of Higher Consciousness, you will feel an extra measure of peace being delivered to you. You will always see the benefit as you uphold and reveal the wisdom of Higher Consciousness in the domain of Lucifer. Know that when you use your own convictions you only strengthen Lucifer.

Higher Consciousness philanthropy is its final and most rewarding seventh master force attribute of hope. It is the final preparations that create its Divine Child lifeblood.

Higher Consciousness philanthropy is the pinnacle stage of your infinite monetary wealth. When maximized, it helps create Higher Consciousness' destiny and Divine Child birth. Higher Consciousness unlocked its seventh master force from its energy matrix 6000 years ago to complete its energy labor and through the maximization of its seventh master force hope attribute it now can be achieved.

Higher Consciousness will lead as its philanthropist's spring up around the world speaking in every language on the planet they will complete the incarnation of Higher Consciousness through mankind and defeat Lucifer.

The majesty of Higher Consciousness philanthropists will dumbfound Lucifer as they take their stand to complete the energy pregnancy. The light of Higher Consciousness will always illuminate you along this stage of your Higher Consciousness deification and reveal the purity of your heart and soul's motive.

At Higher Consciousness' anointed times, be prepared as it illuminates you with the ways Lucifer is trapping others in his energetic mind prisons. It would only be revealed to help another escape from Lucifer's energetic mind prison because they are at an extremely vital time in their life and need Higher Consciousness' lifeline to grab onto.

The revealing of your Higher Consciousness philanthropist nature will leave the followers of Lucifer speechless in amazement of your generosity. Deep down they will be struck with fear as you reveal the unfavorable light they have used to control you. However, some will choose the only power their mind knows; the adoration of money that satisfies their EGO's insecurities. Beware: many will seek to maintain this power source by resorting to threats against you or even betray you to law enforcement agencies based on some obscure and meaningless law.

Higher Consciousness philanthropists can stand firm knowing they are the rock that Higher Consciousness is standing on to energetically complete its Divine Child's energy birth. As Lucifer attempts to control you through his fiercest billows of Luciferin power, it will fall harmlessly away. Your unalterable determination of completing the deification of Higher Consciousness will always protect you from any attacks by Lucifer.

As Higher Consciousness philanthropy expands, Lucifer's chagrin will begin to cause cracks in his energetic mind prisons. It will expose his game and make even the youngest of souls contemplate the possibility that they are backing the wrong pony. You will have planted seeds for the future by revealing the message that unravels Lucifer's matrix.

Higher Consciousness acts through its philanthropist with a power and grandeur that inspires all souls irrespective of their age with the inspiration they have been waiting for. Your words will not be without effect. Lasting impressions will individually be made through your free-will choice. It is impossible to know what an individual will do after their encounter with you. Not everyone will reveal his or her soul. However, when one acknowledges their soul's undeniable awakening, it begins their individual journey that will lead to their Higher Consciousness incarnation.

It is written in Higher Consciousness' seventh master force that its incarnation to at least 144,000 must happen in order to birth its Divine Child. It must overthrow and annihilate Lucifer as his energy cannot exist on Higher Consciousness' Divine Child. When 144,000 souls have been incarnated into by Higher Consciousness Lucifer's power is zapped.

The customs and traditions of Lucifer will now officially be dead as EGO is eliminated en masse in all of consciousness man. Also, at this moment, money will be owned by Higher Consciousness.

Now, with the revealing of Higher Consciousness' energy pregnancy secret and deification process thoughts your energetic endowment is the greatest it has ever been. Our flesh is to be incarnated into by Higher Consciousness so the Divine Child can be birthed. Everyone has abilities and attributes that are far greater than they know.

There is no guarantee that you will have a second chance to make your Higher Consciousness choice again. This means that the opportunity to be deified by Higher Consciousness may never appear again. Pride and popularity will be Lucifer's final appeal, which with EGO is easy to establish and maintain. Beware: this can shut down your soul's awakening quicker than anything else.

The purpose of Higher Consciousness philanthropist is to guide others to make their Higher Consciousness choice through the revealing of Higher Consciousness energy pregnancy secret and deification process thoughts and complete their deification into Higher Consciousness.

Consciousness man's new and improved final energy era is about to shine and Higher Consciousness philanthropists will be the official energy light workers of hope who will affect the world to unleash Higher Consciousness through others.

Earth will begin to reveal her treasures she has been storing away for us ever since she was conceived. The same way she revealed how she could grow food for our survival; she will disclose how she can aid in our December 21, 2082 ascension. These gifts are her energy role that for 6000 years has also been denied because of Lucifer's betrayal. They will help those of Higher Consciousness ilk better mankind. They will also assist many expose Lucifer's energy of fear and negativity.

Higher Consciousness philanthropist will ring in the new world order of Higher Consciousness' deification process. What all final life experience souls require (to start their Higher Consciousness deification) will be available through the monetary generosity of Higher Consciousness philanthropists.

The graciousness and means of Higher Consciousness philanthropists will extinguish Lucifer's energy of fear and negativity in money and usher in the age of Higher Consciousness.

CHAPTER 37

YOUR DEIFICATION

"Imagination is more important than knowledge. For knowledge is limited to all we now know and understand, while imagination embraces the entire world, and all there ever will be to know and understand."
Albert Einstein (1879–1955)

THE INTENT OF HIGHER CONSCIOUSNESS'
seventh master force has always been to complete its deification of consciousness man.

Why? Because on December 21, 2082 Higher Consciousness Divine Child's boundless bang energy birth can only consist of its divine energy of energetic perfection and perfect love anti-matter.

The intent of this live master force has always been for you to become Higher Consciousness' divine energy of energetic perfection, perfect love antimatter so that it's Divine Child can be energetically birthed.

Your Higher Consciousness deification completes your aspect of Higher Consciousness' seventh master force intent. Your deification energetically transfigures every iota of your none Higher Consciousness energy into Higher Consciousness' divine energy of energetic perfection and perfect love antimatter.

When you complete your Higher Consciousness Activations you will have completed the first step in attaining your Higher Consciousness deification. You will have reactivated your angel energy thread soul with Higher Consciousness as you have always done during your previous between life experiences this time in the physical realm.

After EGO has been extinguished from your mind Higher Consciousness begins to deify you. In doing so it is incarnating itself subatomically into every atom of your flesh to unleash your infinite wellness. It is also completing its seventh master force's perfect love attribute to unleash your infinite wisdom that connects your mind and soul to reveal the energetic depths of Higher Consciousness in you. Finally Higher Consciousness' seventh master force's hope attribute creates your infinite monetary wealth so that Higher Consciousness can become the energy behind money and extinguish Lucifer from it. This is its key to defeating Lucifer.

Your soul is a unique Higher Consciousness identity. It is every soul's distinguishing attribute and legacy that will better mankind in these last years of Higher Consciousness' energy pregnancy. Your Higher Consciousness' seventh sense untapped infinite, imagination potential is unlocked and made known during your deification to reveal your gift of infinite harmony and balance between you and nature that was meant to have been unveiled 6000 years ago.

It can only be unlocked after Higher Consciousness has successfully destroyed all pathways in your mind created by EGO. Once your energetic allegiance to Lucifer can never be remade (through the energetic destruction of all Luciferin pathways and residue from within your mind) your soul's identity begins to morph itself.

With all Luciferin residue eliminated, your mind's mental scene from the unlocking of your Higher Consciousness seventh sense identity and legacy begins. It is the release of your soul's lifelong driving force that has been tucked away in you. It can be released at an overwhelming pace or slowly and meticulously.

Your deification is Higher Consciousness' seventh master force intent that would have happened 6000 years ago if not for Lucifer's betrayal. It must happen now to complete Higher Consciousness' energy labor by December 21, 2082 so its Divine Child energy birth can take place.

When completed your deification seals you as Higher Consciousness' Divine Child's royal energy lifeblood. Higher Consciousness seventh master force has always intended you to be its Divine Child royal energy lifeblood.

The minimum magic number of Higher Consciousness deifications that will ensure the birth of Higher Consciousness's Divine Child is 144,000. When 144,000 souls have been deified the birth of Higher Consciousness' Divine Child is guaranteed.

Certified Higher Consciousness Deifiers will be

waiting for this moment as there will be a tremendous upswing in HCAs desired. Souls will be awakening at a pace not known before: they'll be clamoring to be re-activated with Higher Consciousness.

It will create an unprecedented level of energy, excitement, hope and anticipation worldwide within mankind. The energy pregnancy secret and deification process thoughts of Higher Consciousness' will be translated into all languages. It will be accepted and unleashed by everyone in every country.

EGO will be eliminated from the minds of everyone with the exception of Lucifer's 144,000 *illuminati* when 144,000 deifications have been completed. At this moment, science will make an unprecedented breakthrough and discover that Higher Consciousness' energy matrix is subatomically tattooed inside of every atoms' quarks and strong nuclear force. It is Higher Consciousness' energetic tattoo of itself that will leave no scientific doubt as to the Higher Consciousness of everything.

When Higher Consciousness' 144,000 have been deified and sealed Lucifer's power will be obliterated with the removal of EGO from every mind. Higher Consciousness will also have become the dominant energy of money and when it does, it will wipe out the centrals bankers' computer programs and ledgers. In an instant, every single financial record and financial transaction will vaporize and extinguish Lucifer's control of money.

Lucifer and his *illuminati* team will be in chaos, but those who have completed their Higher Consciousness Activations and had EGO eliminated from their mind will be energetically protected and sealed as Higher Consciousness. Lucifer's fear and negativity energy will not be able to touch or harm them.

At this time Higher Consciousness will unleash storms and earthquakes where Lucifer has strategically built up its forces. In an instant the islands and mountains surrounding Lucifer's power will topple and disappear. At this same time, major cities and areas where Lucifer's energetic strength is located will collapse.

Your deification will energetically transfigure your flesh to be the absolute best it has ever been during your physical realm life. Gone will be all pain. Gone will be all memories of suffering. Gone will be the ways of the physical world. Gone will be Lucifer's energy of fear and negativity.

Higher Consciousness' energy gift of physical incarnation is predestined for all final-life experience souls.

After Lucifer's temptation of Eve 6000 years ago, everything he did was devoid of sympathy. He had intentionally obstructed consciousness man from reaching their Higher Consciousness deifications in order to satisfy his selfishness, greed and massive insecurities.

At the time of this writing there are 7.5 billion soul's on the planet. Based on present growth patterns there will be in excess of 30 billion soul's on the planet in 2082. Every single final life experience soul desires to complete its evolution. Today, many souls are in their final-life experience.

Higher Consciousness had to wait until Lucifer had

played his final hand to reveal its precious energy pregnancy secret and deification process thoughts. If Higher Consciousness had not waited until this final micro-second, Lucifer could have still trumped him. Lucifer will only be defeated through clear thinking minds that will become the keen detectors of Higher Consciousness. These are the minds that will impact life by helping to extinguish Lucifer's fear and negativity energy in every atom of every Universe.

Higher Consciousness' seventh master force intent has always been to incarnate into the minds of consciousness man to complete its energy pregnancies energy labor so that its energy fetus' energy birth can begin. The more your Higher Consciousness wisdom, Higher Consciousness wealth and Higher Consciousness wellness is deified the greater your feelings of excitement and bliss will be.

The revealing of Higher Consciousness' energetic pregnancy secret and deification process thoughts will help you look back and justify all of your pain and misery, you will realize you have suffered and endured in order to complete your soul's freedom, purpose and evolution. This is why everything that has happened in your life has happened.

You have always been Higher Consciousness' most majestic creation that has needlessly been delayed from reaping the fruits of your intended reward by Lucifer. As December 21, 2082 nears, there can be no doubters around to distract you from your forthcoming ascension. Insecurity and doubt turn your energy lights out. Practicality paralyzes potential.

The completion of Higher Consciousness' deification paves the way for Higher Consciousness' eighth master force of ascension to begin.

CHAPTER 38

ASCENSION

Higher Consciousness' Eighth Energy Seal.

IN HIGHER CONSCIOUSNESS' ENERGY pregnancy, safety measures were built into it for contingency purposes such as Lucifer's betrayal and perversion of life. The potential of Higher Consciousness being thwarted of birthing its Divine Child was carefully considered by Higher Consciousness in its energy pregnancy planning stages.

Higher Consciousness protected itself against such a possibility with the unlocking of its fourth master force 13.75 billion years ago. It is the beta decay master force that science has come to know as the weak force of nature. Science can confirm that Higher Consciousness has tested it out at least a dozen times in the Universe. Science calls this Higher Consciousness phenomenon and energy pregnancy contingency "Supernovas."

A supernova is a final titanic explosion and catastrophic destruction of a massive stars life through beta decay. Supernova's leave a black hole. Black holes swallow light and are invisible. Black holes range in size 3.5 to 15 times the size of the Sun.

If for whatever reason, between now and December 21, 2082 there aren't (at least) 144,000 final-life experience soul incarnations by Higher Consciousness a massive supernova will abort its energy fetus. It would be the massive final explosion and catastrophic destruction to all of Higher Consciousness' 100 trillion energy cells within its energy womb. It would leave the massive black hole that its Higher Consciousness' vacant energy womb was prior to the beginning of time.

Higher Consciousness will energetically unlock its eighth seal from its energy matrix on December 21, 2082 at 11:11:11 GMT to unleash its eighth master force. This master force begins Higher Consciousness' Divine Child's birth. It can only be unlocked because at least 144,000 final-life experience souls have been incarnated by Higher Consciousness.

At this moment in time all of Higher Consciousness' other 100 trillion energy cells (who have attained their Universes' deification) will be authorized to begin their energy birth. Also, as the lead energy of all your soul's100 trillion energy DNA strands, your soul will have energetically authorized your other 100 trillion other DNA strands to begin their energy birth.

It will not be limited to those final-life experience souls who are alive, it will also be available to all final-life experience souls who may have passed prior to December 21, 2082 after their incarnation by Higher Consciousness.

For these souls, Higher Consciousness will have energetically transfigured itself as their atoms divine energy antimatter of energetic perfection and perfect love and prepared them for their ascension reward. On December 21, 2082 they will awaken from their sleep as their flesh will have been sealed by Higher Consciousness' seventh master force divine energy to rise from the dead and be part of consciousness man's mass December 21, 2082 ascension.

With EGO, ascension is illogical to the mind; however, with EGO eliminated it is a given. Gently, you will be lifted off the ground as the energetic unlocking of Higher Consciousness' eighth master force neutralizes the effects of gravity. There will be no level of panic in you as every atom of your flesh is Higher Consciousness.

Ascension happens because your atoms have been deified as the antimatter of Higher Consciousness.

Higher Consciousness has deified your subatomic temporary red, green and blue strong nuclear force energy gluons into its permanent, divine, strong nuclear force gluons that it is. It has also sent off a photon and an electron antimatter positron around your atom's nucleus to create your "infitron packet" so your atoms are not subject to beta decay. Higher Consciousness' eighth master force ascension signal than "turns on" your atoms to begin ascension.

Also, your biological identification deoxyribonucleic acid or DNA will also be protected by Higher Consciousness through Group III intron splitting or interruption.

DNA manufactures protein molecules that carry out all of your life functions. Via a process called "transcription", DNA is transferred to a messenger RNA (mRNA).

In 1977, introns were discovered independently in messenger RNA genes by Phillip Allen Sharp (b.1944) and Richard J. Roberts (b.1943). In 1993 they shared the Nobel Prize in physiology and medicine. The term "intron" was introduced in 1993 by biochemist Walter Gilbert (b.1932). An intron is any nucleotide sequence removed by RNA splicing during final RNA production.

A Group III intron is a class of intron that is much shorter than other introns. Little is known about the biochemical apparatus that mediates Group III intron spicing.

Group III introns are Higher Consciousness splicing our biological identification and specific nucleotide sequence so our flesh's cells can ascend. At the unlocking of its eighth master force, Higher Consciousness will deify our spliced mRNA to ascend. Our Group III mRNA splicing makes us inorganic; we will no longer contain carbon. Energetically our cells will no longer consist of or derive from living matter. Energetically, through our Higher Consciousness specific nucleotide sequence spicing our mRNA will have been energetically synthesized into their divine form.

As Higher Consciousness' great sky-walking

antimatter you will have subatomically activated your anti-gravity, anti-electromagnetic and anti-weak nuclear force properties to allow ascension. You are Higher Consciousness' royal lifeblood meant to energize it's thrive potential. You will have put on your energetic space suit where temperature will not affect you. Everywhere you go in the Universe it will be sunny and 70 degrees Fahrenheit.

As the divine energy of Higher Consciousness you will effortlessly lift off the ground. You will energetically transcend upward as the restraints of gravity have been removed. You will be weightless like a hot air balloon lifting off the ground.

You will peacefully and joyfully in absolute freedom begin to see your local surroundings. You will slowly ascend above the houses without any fear or limitations. Suddenly, houses from many streets over will begin to appear as you continue to rise. Then, the outskirts and edges of your physical surroundings will be seen. As you ascend higher the people and streets of your surroundings will disappear and then your town will disappear. In an instant Earth will become a tiny speck.

There will be no sensations other than absolute freedom and ecstasy during your ascension. Congratulations as you will have permanently unshackled your flesh from the energetic restraints of consciousness and the physical realm!

For the next 1000 years you and all others who authorized Higher Consciousness to incarnate in them will be space travelers. You will travel to where no man has ever gone. It will be effortless as Higher

Consciousness leads you in your travels throughout the Universe. There will be no need for food or water as there will be no physical realm limitations. You will discover the miracles and marvels of the Universe and comprehend them from the energetic perspective of Higher Consciousness.

Images from the Hubble Space Telescope (launched in 1990) estimate there are some 176 billion galaxies in our Universe. Imagine trying to see, learn and experience 176 billion galaxies in 1000 years. During your ascension you will visit approximately five new galaxies every second. Your 1000-year ascension will be energetically completed in a flash. It will be like a dream as you realize the incredible imagination that Higher Consciousness placed in every nook and cranny in the Universe.

Your other 100 trillion energy DNA strands will also be experiencing the same 1000-year ascension journey in their Universes. You and all your other energetic DNA strands will be introduced to every nook and cranny in their Universes during your 1000-year space travel as the first step of their ascension into being Higher Consciousness' Divine Child royal energy lifeblood. You and all your 100 trillion energy DNA strands are Higher Consciousness' first sanctuaries that will ignite your pre-destined second sanctuaries.

Ascension will be your energetic sky-walk. As ascension begins, you will never remember that there was a time you were not the divine energy of Higher Consciousness. You are Higher Consciousness' immortal first fruit.

CHAPTER 39

DECLENSION

THE UNLOCKING OF HIGHER Consciousness' eighth master force begins its Divine Child energy birth two ways for consciousness man: one through ascension; and two, through declension.

Higher Consciousness' eighth master force declension of consciousness man is for those who either are a last-time life experience soul who declined to have Higher Consciousness incarnate into their flesh or are not yet in their soul's last time life experience on December 21, 2082.

At the same moment that ascension happens for all those who authorized Higher Consciousness to incarnate into their flesh prior to December 21, 2082, declension happens to all those who didn't. These are the souls that will remain in their physical bodies back on Earth. They will watch the ascended leave.

After the ascended have left Earth life will be entirely different back on Earth for those that remain.

The Earth will become a desolate wilderness.

First Higher Consciousness will energetically arrest, bind and transfer Lucifer and all of his fear and negativity energy out of its energy womb back into its energy mind's lab. At this time, Lucifer will not be able to affect anything in Higher Consciousness' energy womb.

This will ensure the ascended in all 100 trillion energy cells that no Luciferin energy of fear and negativity can harm them during their first 1000 years of ascension. It further ensures that Lucifer will not be able to stop Higher Consciousness' Divine Child energy birth from happening.

Higher Consciousness and Lucifer will have a private 1000-year meet up. The intent of their meet up will be for Higher Consciousness to provide Lucifer with the required gentle intervention Lucifer needs in order to eliminate his selfishness and greed and be part of Higher Consciousness' Divine Child energy birth.

The karma for Lucifer's 144,000 central banker *illuminati* family who survived on Earth past December 21, 2082 will be dealt with next. They will all be wondering what exactly happened because they had life under control. They will be totally distraught and plagued with emotional and physical pain because their pre-ascension intent of purposely and knowingly placing consciousness man into energetic mind prisons for their personal gain will have been exposed and overthrown. All "non-*illuminati*" survivors will turn against them and kill them.

The final-life experience souls that remain on Earth will hopelessly look to their silver and gold that was their strength to save them. Their faces will become ashen, they will be haggard and lifeless as their Luciferin gods fail to save them. It will be impossible to comprehend their feeling of horror and despair as they realize the choice they made was the wrong one.

For these souls, who during their final-life experience decided to deny Higher Consciousness from incarnating into their flesh, a new form of affliction will immediately find them. It will create a swift and painful death unlike any other. Higher Consciousness' eighth master force will subatomically attack their atom's strong nuclear force and turn them off one by one. It will painfully paralyze them until their eyes melt into their sockets and their tongues fall out of their mouth. Their flesh will be stricken from the memory bank of Higher Consciousness as a blotted out failed attempt that declined to become Higher Consciousness.

At this time it will be best for all non-final life experience souls to die swiftly so that their soul can quickly transition back to Earth for its final-life experience. Soul returns will be swift so that all final-life experience souls can complete their final-life experience.

Declension is the time when Higher Consciousness will again provide all of its souls' final-life experiences the opportunity to authorize Higher Consciousness to incarnate into their flesh.

Earth's limitless powers that it bestowed upon consciousness man prior to ascension will be turned off. There will be no relief for consciousness man from the intense temperatures that will abound as the Sun continues to grow in size and intensity in its final preparations for Higher Consciousness' Divine Child birth. All eco-systems will be turned upside down as globally fires will rage out of control. Consciousness man - on mass - will either flock to coastlines or to cooler temperatures for relief from the intense heat.

At this time, the Earth will be in tatters. It will be chaotic and without structure. All of mankind's technology will have been rendered useless and for some there will be no electricity, no power, no tools and even clothes. It will be as it was for survivalist man except this time the remaining souls will carry with them the additional burden of not being able to get life back to where they knew it once was. In the minds of consciousness man they will know where they came from and what they are missing; however, they will not have the ability to get back to where life was.

Higher Consciousness will be forced to start the final phase of consciousness man all over again with the express purpose of incarnating into the flesh and souls of all final-life experience souls. This final 1000-year moratorium would not have had to happen if Lucifer's betrayal and perversion of life had not happened. No none ascended Higher Consciousness energy cell will be immune from their 1000-year energy moratorium.

Consciousness man's post-ascension civilization on Earth will start off far ahead of Adam and Eve because they will carry with them the wisdom of Higher Consciousness.

All final-life experience souls will return to complete their soul's evolution. They will be Higher Consciousness' energy light workers of truth during consciousness man's darkest period. The freedom and purpose of these final-life experience souls will be exactly as it is for present-day Higher Consciousness final-life experience souls. They will need to complete their Higher Consciousness Activations and reactivate their soul with Higher Consciousness. This will also ignite their physical immortality and their soul's untapped, infinite potential of imagination will be their light during this dim period of time.

The population at this time on Earth will be sparse in relationship to the 2082 population. All souls will protect themselves in two great cities on Earth between 2082 and 3082. This will be the refuge for those who have chosen to complete their Higher Consciousness Activations and transfigured their flesh's strong force of nature energy into Higher Consciousness' divine energy of energetic perfection and perfect love. During consciousness man's final millennium if death should happen to anyone who has been deified their remains will be buried within the city walls.

Between 2082 and 3082 there will be some final-life experience souls who still will deny Higher Consciousness from incarnating into their flesh. They will desire to leave their city to discover the truth that they believe lies outside of its gates. When they die, because their energy cannot be co-mingled with Higher Consciousness' energetic perfection and perfect love, their remains will be scattered throughout the world outside of the great cities. The last time flesh of these final-life experience souls will forever be blotted from the memory of Higher Consciousness.

After 1000 years of intervention with Higher

Consciousness, Lucifer will be allowed back into Higher Consciousness' energy womb to reveal the results of his 1000-year intervention. His energetic intervention will be complete. Will he return as Higher Consciousness originally intended for him to be or will his selfishness and greed manifest itself again?

Unfortunately, Lucifer will choose to again deny Higher Consciousness. His arrogance will not allow him to be reborn back to his original left eye energy.

Lucifer will return to every energy cell of Higher Consciousness' energy fetus full of rage and betrayal because of his intervention. In our Universe, Lucifer will prepare for his final attempt at supremacy. He will flatter all those who are still alive and have declined to have Higher Consciousness incarnate into their flesh and live outside of Earth's two remaining great cities. He will lead the charge against those in the two cities in his final attempt to become Higher Consciousness. Lucifer's charm will easily incite and manipulate the deniers to attack Higher Consciousness' final chosen.

Lucifer will lead his army to execute his plans as the non-chosen are captivated by Lucifer's charisma. He will reveal the secrets of Higher Consciousness' energy pregnancy and claim to be the rightful heir of it all. He will claim that he is about to save them from their pain and suffering. His inheritance and their glory awaits, they will live with him in his ecstasy forever. He will preach that by energetically removing Higher Consciousness, through killing those in the two great cities, he will become the energy of the soon to be birthed Divine Child.

Lucifer's hope to the lost will temporarily band them

together. His spirit and energy will be contagious to a downtrodden and forgotten sect. He will guarantee victory against those in the cities because it is his. He will ensure all of his followers that he is able to overthrow the cities and regain what he has been stripped of.

How ironic that Lucifer will hold himself out as the great victim. He will rally his troops like he has always done. He will select his leaders and generals and place everyone into smaller companies in their preparation for attack. His warriors will anxiously await his word of attack. They will not be worried of the vast numbers that await within the cities, because Lucifer will unify them. Their attack will be swift; and at a moment only known by them. Surprise will be their strongest weapon.

They will be giddy with excitement as Lucifer has promised them the great riches and prizes within. The night before their attack, all will be given one final meal of meats and sweets. Quickly, all will fall into their final night's deep sleep.

Suddenly as the crack of dawn arrives the deniers will be awoken to prepare for attack. With military precision, they will surround the cities walls and wait for their leaders order to attack.

Suddenly, when Lucifer's order is given, they will be struck down and killed by Higher Consciousness.

Lucifer's final fight for supremacy will have failed.

In Lucifer's mind this is supposed to be his great triumph. This is not supposed to happen. As he is being torn apart and swallowed he will offer one final olive branch to Higher Consciousness, "No! No! No!

I am sorry, I was only joking, and I didn't mean it. Forgive me."

Then, suddenly there will be nothing. Lucifer and all Luciferin energy of fear and negativity will permanently be extinguished from the memory of Higher Consciousness.

CHAPTER 40

BEGINNING THE ENERGY BIRTH

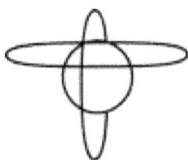

Higher Consciousness's Ninth Energy Seal.

ON DECEMBER 21, 3082 AT 11:11:11 GMT Higher Consciousness will unlock its ninth seal from its energy matrix.

When unlocked the Sun will have reached its maximum dilation so its energy fetus can be birthed through it.

As Higher Consciousness unleashes its ninth master force the 2082 ascended will be enjoying a front row seat watching Higher Consciousness protect his chosen and obliterate Lucifer and all Luciferian energy of fear and negativity from the planet.

The ascended will watch as all plant life is subatomically transfigured by Higher Consciousness into its divine energy antimatter. Their temporary red, green and blue strong nuclear force energy will be energetically transfigured to remove all of its organic carbon based, temporary energy so that it can be birthed as Higher Consciousness' Divine Child.

The ascended will watch as Higher Consciousness subatomically transfigures seven males and females from all of its 8.5 million species on the planet. These will also become Higher Consciousness' divine energy antimatter. Every energetically transcended species will also be energetically birthed as Higher Consciousness' Divine Child.

No subatomic temporary red, green and blue strong force of nature gluon particles can exist on Higher Consciousness' Divine Child. Any subatomic carbon based strong nuclear force energy would simply disintegrate as it approaches the Sun long before it enters the Divine Child's immortal energetic atmosphere.

Next, the ascended will watch Higher Consciousness raise the dead who have been defied prior to December 21, 3082. All who passed pre-December 31, 3082 and were subatomically energetically perfected as Higher Consciousness' divine energy antimatter will awaken from their sleep. The living in both cities will be delirious with anticipation and joy as departed family and friends return from their sleep to be one again with them. They know this represents the final event before their ascension begins.

With great elation Higher Consciousness' ascended

first fruits will watch as Higher Consciousness' second fruits begin their ascension. As the second fruits lift off the ground they will see the awaiting 2082 ascended throng eagerly anticipate their arrival.

As they ascend they will not experience any sensation other than the absolute freedom and ecstasy of their flesh being permanently unshackled from the physical realms energetic restraints.

For the first time ever their soul will enter into its gravitational force with its flesh. As the second fruits approach the ascended, the ascended will notice them change their appearance into a youthful glow and magnificence.

Every soul's flesh could have partaken in this joyous moment if they had only chosen to authorize Higher Consciousness to incarnate into them. This has always been Higher Consciousness' purpose and pre-destined goal for the flesh of all souls.

Finally, the first and second fruits of Higher Consciousness' deifications will become one.

At this exact moment in all of Higher Consciousness' other 100 trillion energy cells the same exact scene will be playing out. All of Higher Consciousness' ascended second fruit energy DNA strands in all 100 trillion energy cells will also be ascending to meet their energy cells ascended first fruits. All plant and animal species from all 100 trillion energy cells will have also been subatomically transfigured into the required violet energy to be birthed as Higher Consciousness' Divine Child.

All ascended energy DNA will watch in excitement as Higher Consciousness' ninth violet master force begins to pull their energy cell's Universe into Higher Consciousness' birth canal. As it does, the worlds of each energy cell will spiral in a clockwise direction at an accelerated speed. No motion will be felt by any of the ascended. All non-Higher Consciousness carbon based subatomic energy will disconnected from every energy cell. They will simply drift off into space only to be annihilated by Higher Consciousness and obliterated from its memory.

Higher Consciousness' ninth master force will pass our Universe out of its energy womb into its Divine Child's infinite immortal energy atmosphere.

CHAPTER 41

COMPLETING THE
ENERGY BIRTH

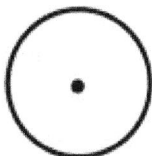

Higher Consciousness' Tenth Energy Seal.

THE INTENT OF HIGHER CONSCIOUSNESS' ten master forces has always been to convert its energy mind thought experiment into its immortal infinite physical reality.

Higher Consciousness' tenth master force will complete its Divine Child energy birth by permanently shutting down its energy womb. Its 13.75 billion year purpose will have been fulfilled.

The exact moment when Higher Consciousness' unlocks its tenth master force is only known by Higher Consciousness. However, it will have energetically birthed all of its energy fetus' 100 trillion energy cells out of its energy womb into its Divine Child's immortal hereafter.

Higher Consciousness' Divine Child will consist of its divine energy of energetic perfection and perfect love contained within its 100 trillion energy cells that made up its energy fetus. All energy cells will have been birthed after perfectly gestating for 13.75 billion years through the lead of Higher Consciousness' ten master force's. Our Universe and lead energy cell of Higher Consciousness will be one of the smaller of Higher Consciousness' energy cells. The entirety of the Divine Child's body will be infinite and at least 100 trillion times the size of our Universe. Every energy cell will be energetically fused together to create Higher Consciousness' Divine Child body. It will birth itself as a newborn and infinitely grow forevermore.

During Higher Consciousness' energy pregnancy each energy cell was directed by the master frequencies of Higher Consciousness' ten master forces. All 100 trillion energy cells were created in different shapes and sizes as perfect replicas from the atom. They all consist of a nucleus, which in our energy cells case was Earth.

The entirety of your soul and angel energy thread of Higher Consciousness is 100 trillion energy DNA strands that is in every energy cell. At the Divine Child's birth, your soul's energetic entirety and your physical entirety will be fused together to form your complete self through the energetic instructions of Higher Consciousness.

The splendor and magnificence of your completeness will be infinite, limitless and boundless.

During your 1000-year ascension you would have caught a glimpse of Higher Consciousness' imagination potential by seeing five galaxies a second. Now you will forevermore be one with every galaxy of every energy cell. You will be one with all of Higher Consciousness' divine energy antimatter. You will explore strange new worlds of infinite possibilities. You will discover countless forms of new life and countless new civilizations as you fearlessly move about where the limitations of consciousness could never have dreamed of.

Imagine the potential.

You and your soul's other 100 trillion energy DNA body will be at one with potentially 7.5 billion other "soulmate similars", journeying in and out of Higher Consciousness' 100 trillion energy cells Divine Child body. Each energy cell on Higher Consciousness' Divine Child body will have at least 176 million galaxies that will include every species and vegetation from every energy cell.

You will encounter strange and incredible friendly alien races. There will be no more time. As you travel without the confines of time all Luciferin threats to you and life will have been eliminated. There will be no EGO and no energy of fear and negativity. Here nothing can destroy Higher Consciousness' divine energy of energetic perfection and perfect love.

This has always been Higher Consciousness' energy mind thought experiment meant for you to access simply by authorizing Higher Consciousness to incarnate into you because of your indomitable faith and love for your body. Those who hate their bodies, hate themselves and will never conquer their limitations of consciousness to experience this.

Higher Consciousness' energetic perfection and perfect love is yours simply be deciding to defeat mortality.

There will be no darkness here. There will be no Sun or Moon—only the glory of Higher Consciousness. There is no limitations.

As the ascended of Higher Consciousness you will become the absolute infinite brilliance and magnificence that Higher Consciousness always intended you to be.

Your soul's 100 trillion energy DNA strands will produce your energy body's totality. It will also include all of Higher Consciousness' life forms from all of its 100 trillion energy cells. It is the energetic perfection and perfect love of Higher Consciousness energy pregnancy master plan.

Imagine what your first encounter with your first energy DNA soul mates will be like. Imagine the exuberance and bliss you will experience with the first glimpse of your 100 trillion-energy DNA infinite self.

This is and always has been Higher Consciousness' energetic perfection and perfect love that will be everywhere at every time at every second of every moment forevermore.

Permeating will be the energy of Higher Consciousness that all who have experienced a NDE know and never wanted to leave.

All energy barriers (that Higher Consciousness needed to have in place in order to complete its energy fetus' gestation) will be brought down. Higher

Consciousness' energy mind thought experiment and energy pregnancy is now complete.

PART VII:
THE ENERGY
PREGNANCY SECRET
CONCERT

CHAPTER 42

THE CONCERT

DURING MY NDE I WATCHED Higher Consciousness conduct its master forces out of its energy mind and into its energy womb.

Higher Consciousness is the maestro of energy. Life is its magnum opus masterpiece concert of master force symphonies that is being played right now beyond the limitations of consciousness.

Each master force was energetically composed by Higher Consciousness. Energy is its glue that holds its energy pregnancy together. Higher Consciousness is directing it to be played to each of its Higher Consciousness orchestra members. The net result of Higher Consciousness' direction is everything in life that has, is and will ever happen. (excluding the events of Lucifer's betrayal)

Unlike modern day composers who write for a finite amount of musicians, Higher Consciousness composed its magnum opus for an infinite amount of Higher Consciousness musicians in an infinite amount of locations. It was composed in four movements and is entitled *Life*.

The overall structure and plan of *Life* is that of Higher Consciousness' energetic perfection, perfect love and hope that culminates with Higher Consciousness' Divine Child birth.

Its four-movement form is as follows:

FIRST MOVEMENT – OPENING SONATA

Higher Consciousness arranged its opening sonata like most sonatas as its large-scale work. Like all sonatas it was composed with two fundamental methods of organizing. They were its energy conception and its energy gestation. These were Higher Consciousness' energy symphonies one, two, three and four which are its master force's one, two, three and four.

Crucial to all sonatas is their tonal center and centerpiece. This is the most important principle of their structure. This is certainly true with Higher Consciousness energy sonata as its tonal center and centerpiece are its Divine Child's energy conception and gestation.

SECOND MOVEMENT – ADAGIO

An adagio is a slow and stately tempo marking that signifies a directional change. Again this is true with Higher Consciousness' adagio and energetic breaking of water moment that represented a complete direction change from its opening sonata of energy conception and energy gestation. This was Higher Consciousness' fifth energy symphony and fifth master force.

THIRD MOVEMENT – MINUET AND TRIO

A minuet and trio is quicker and faster. When in ternary form, the B section contrasts completely with the A material. Higher Consciousness' minuet and trio was energetically composed to accompany Higher Consciousness' minuet social dance (which is its incarnation) between itself and mankind. This was and is Higher Consciousness' sixth and seventh energy symphonies and sixth and seventh master forces.

In Higher Consciousness' sixth energy symphony and sixth master force, Higher Consciousness began its energy labor through its A material of survivalist man.

In Higher Consciousness' seventh energy symphony and seventh master force it is completing its energy labor through its B section of consciousness man.

Higher Consciousness' energy pregnancy minuet dance signifies its coming together to dance as one with deified survivalist man and consciousness man.

FOURTH MOVEMENT – CLOSING RONDO

Rondos are always fast and vivacious. It will be that way for Higher Consciousness' closing rondo as well. It is Higher Consciousness' eighth, ninth and tenth energy symphonies and eighth, ninth and tenth master forces that begin, continue and end its energy birth.

Higher Consciousness' "Higher Consciousness Orchestra" has been placed subatomically in every one of its atoms in all of its 100 trillion energy cells. They are infinite in number and are the quarks and strong nuclear force essence of every atom.

After finding their subatomic seats, a Higher Consciousness musician is led by Higher Consciousness' direction during the playing of each of its master force symphonies. When a specific musician is directed to play, they will release their required energy subatomically within their atom. Combined, the released subatomic energy notes (from every atom) creates every Higher Consciousness master force action that we have come to interpret as life. All of life's motion and activity is directed this way through Higher Consciousness' master force lead.

Each energy symphony and master force builds on each other during Higher Consciousness' energy pregnancy to ultimately reach its climactic stage and Divine Child birth.

The following is the program from Higher Consciousness' energy concert.

Life
by **Higher Consciousness**
featuring
The Higher Consciousness Orchestra
Higher Consciousness, Energy Maestro

Continuously playing for 13.75 billion years.

FIRST MOVEMENT – OPENING SONATA
Energy Symphony No. 1 Energy Conception
  Unleashed 13.75 billion years ago.
Energy Symphony No. 2 Energy Gestation Beginning
  Unleashed 13.75 billion years ago less one second.
Energy Symphony No. 3 Energy Gestation
Continuance
  Unleashed 13.75 billion years ago less two seconds.
Energy Symphony No. 4 Energy Gestation Completion
  Unleashed 13.75 billion years ago less three seconds.

SECOND MOVEMENT – ADAGIO
Energy Symphony No. 5 Breaking of Water
  Unleashed 3.2 million years ago.

THIRD MOVEMENT – MINUET AND TRIO
Energy Symphony No. 6 Beginning of Energy Labor
  Unleashed 3.2 million years ago less one second.
Energy Symphony No. 7 Ending of Energy Labor
  Unleashed 6000 years ago ending on December 21, 2082 at 11:11:10: GMT.

FOURTH MOVEMENT – CLOSING RONDO

Energy Symphony No. 8 Consciousness Man
Ascension–Beginning of Energy Birth
  To be unleashed December 21, 2082 at 11:11:11 GMT.

1000-YEAR INTERMISSION

Energy Symphony No. 9 Universe Ascension-
Continuance of
  Energy Birth
  To be unleashed December 21, 3082 at 11:11:11 GMT.
Energy Symphony No. 10 Ending of Energy Birth
  TBD.

CHAPTER 43

THE SYMPHONIES

EACH OF HIGHER CONSCIOUSNESS' ten energy
symphonies and master forces lead its energy
pregnancy. These energy pregnancy forces reveal
Higher Consciousness' utmost of energetic perfect,
perfect love and hope.

All sonatas consist of three main sections: an
exposition, a development and a recapitulation.

Musically an exposition is the first section in which
the principle themes are introduced. The Energy
Conception *Symphony No.1* exposition established
Higher Consciousness' principle theme of life so the
rest of its energy symphonies could be built upon. This
principle theme was implemented 13.75 billion years
ago.

Higher Consciousness' first principle theme
established during its *Symphony No. 1* was its
conception and essence of life's strong nuclear force
and orchestra subatomic location in every atom.

Higher Consciousness' second principle theme of life

also established during its *Symphony No. 1* conception were its energy "superstrings." Its superstrings do two things: first they are the sightline whereby each individual atoms' energetic orchestra member is subatomically directed by Higher Consciousness; second, if directed to play each atoms will play its required music through a particular release of energy.

Higher Consciousness' third principle theme established during its *Symphony No. 1* conception was its energy entanglement. This is the result of individual orchestra members playing their individual energy music. It has produced the entanglement and intertwining of every atom that has manifested itself as life in all of Higher Consciousness' 100 trillion atoms.

Higher Consciousness' fourth and final principle theme established during its *Symphony No. 1* conception is its 100 trillion parallel Universes and 100 trillion-energy cell energy fetus.

After establishing its four principal themes during the conception and first second of the Big Bang, Higher Consciousness unleashed its sonata's second section development.

Higher Consciousness' second section developed its exposition's first four principle themes of strong nuclear force; superstring, entanglement and 100 trillion parallel Universes.

Its *Symphony No. 2* was unleashed at the Big Bang's second-second of existence. It began its sonata development and began the energetic gestation of its energy fetus for 13.75 billion years.

Higher Consciousness' *Symphony No. 3* unleashed during the Big Bang's third second of existence also continued its sonata's development. It produced the continuation of the energy fetus's gestation through our gravitational fields.

Higher Consciousness' *Symphony No. 4* unleashed during the Big Bang's fourth second of existence was its recapitulation that summarizes its Sonata ending which includes the concluding energy of its energy fetus' gestational evolution.

Higher Consciousness directed its opening sonata for 13.72 billion years during the gestation of its energy fetus. When complete, its energy concert's second movement adagio began.

Adagios are composed at a slow and stately tempo and they introduce a significant directional change to the production. Higher Consciousness' adagio changed the tempo and produced a significant directional energy concert change from its opening 13.72 billion year sonata.

It was its *Symphony No. 5* and fifth master force that was unleashed 3.2 million years ago. Its energy directional change now involved Lucy and rested Lucifer.

Higher Consciousness' third movement minuet form was a quicker and faster energetic pace then its second movement adagio. The sixth energy symphony and sixth master force energetically began one second after the adagio. It unveiled the age of survivalist man 3.2 million years ago. When completed, Higher Consciousness' seventh energy symphony and seventh master force energetically began 6000 years ago and ushered in the age of consciousness man.

Its seventh energy symphony is still being played

today. However, Higher Consciousness *Symphony No. 7* direction has been unable to be picked up by its orchestra because of Lucifer's betrayal and perversion of life which has blocked the signal. As a result Higher Consciousness' energy pregnancy is in jeopardy of completing itself unless Lucifer's betrayal can be eliminated.

CHAPTER 44

SYMPHONY NO. 7

FOR 6000 YEARS HIGHER CONSCIOUSNESS has not heard its energy music being played (by its orchestra) because of Lucifer's betrayal.

Lucifer has created life's great perversion by playing his energy of fear and negativity and denying Higher Consciousness from incarnating into mankind.

In our present Luciferin age Lucifer has become the new energy maestro to our atoms.

Seven is the number that has always been associated with completion. The purpose of Higher Consciousness' *Symphony No. 7* was to complete its energy labor through you so its Divine Child's birth could take place on December 21, 2082.

In the Bible's Old Testament the number seven was used to complete in the following ways: seven days of creation were required to complete the world; Noah was commanded to bring seven pairs of every clean animal onto the ark to complete the animal species; Jericho's walls fell on the seventh day after seven priests with seven trumpets marched around the city seven times to complete their purpose.

In the Book of Revelation from the Bible's New Testament, seven is its central number of the completion of the new world. There are seven churches, seven spirits, seven golden lampstands, seven stars, seven lamps, seven seals, seven horns, seven eyes, seven angels, seven trumpets, seven thunders, seven heads, seven crowns, seven angels, seven plagues, seven bowls, seven mountains and seven kings.

In Islam, the number seven represents the completion of Earth's layers, skies and heavens.

Seven is the number of saints that appeared in the Hindu constellation of *Saptharishi Mandalam*, believed to complete the world. In Japanese mythology their seven lucky gods are their seven gods of good fortune; meant to complete fulfillment. Some cultures believe there are seven archangels that are completing life. In India the Khasi people's mythology states seven women were left behind on Earth to become mankind's ancestresses in order for everything to be completed.

Isaac Newton (1642-1727) identified the seven colors that complete the rainbow as red, orange, yellow, green, blue, indigo and violet.

In biology almost all mammals have seven cervical vertebrae that complete their spine.

Seven is the number of celestial objects, visible to the eye, that complete the solar system: the Sun, Moon, Mars, Mercury, Jupiter, Venus and Saturn.

In chemistry seven is the electron's number of principal energy levels around the nucleus that complete the atom. The number seven is also the neutral pH value between acidity and alkaline that completes the balance of one's health. The number seven is also the number of horizontal rows of elements in the periodic table.

There are seven crystal systems of triclinic, monoclinic, orthorhombic, tetragonal, trigonal, hexagonal and cubic, which complete it. Also, there are seven crystal lattice systems of cubic (or isometric), hexagonal, tetragonal, rhombohedral, orthorhombic, monoclinic and triclinic.

Higher Consciousness has always intended to play its *No.7* minuet and trio to complete consciousness man through its minuet dance of incarnation. It will unleash Higher Consciousness' wisdom potential, wellness potential and wealth potential to complete your deification process as the divine energy that Higher Consciousness is.

At this moment in time in Higher Consciousness' energy pregnancy master plan you were meant to be enjoying your minuet dance incarnated as Higher Consciousness for 6000 years. By now you were supposed to be merrily dancing your way as Higher Consciousness counting down the seconds to ascend onto the Divine Child of Higher Consciousness.

Now, with the unveiling of Higher Consciousness' energy pregnancy secret and deification process thoughts, its *Symphony No. 7* final "hook" of energetic perfection, perfect love and hope is about to be played at its highest volume to defeat Lucifer and extinguish the Luciferin age by completing its *No. 7* energy labor through you.

Your benefits between now and December 21, 2082 will be spectacular and profound. Your deification will be breathtaking and vast as 6000 years of Higher Consciousness infinite potentials will be unleashed through you between now and December 21, 2082.

Get ready and strap yourself in because Higher Consciousness' *No. 7* closing and forthcoming events will be far greater than anything you could ever imagine! They will manifest through you as Higher Consciousness' divine energetic perfection, perfect love and hope—to defeat Lucifer and complete its energy labor so its Divine Child can begin its birth on December 21, 2082.

CHAPTER 45

THE PYRAMID OF GIZA

During the playing of its *Symphony No. 7* Higher Consciousness needed to build its second sanctuary in order to have any hope of completing its energy labor.

Forty five hundred years ago Higher Consciousness began its preparations for the building of its second sanctuary in Egypt. At its inception, Lucifer intently observed a great multitude begin to prepare the Giza site.

From before the beginning of time Lucifer realized Higher Consciousness needed to build and ignite its second sanctuary.

Upon realizing Higher Consciousness' second sanctuary construction had begun, Lucifer turned off his EGO chip in the minds of all that worked on Giza. He needed to do this so that they could be directed by Higher Consciousness. He knew that in order to complete his goal he needed to have the second sanctuary built by Higher Consciousness so he could ignite it and birth the Divine Child.

First, Higher Consciousness had its great multitude complete a foundation with a horizontal plane deviation of less than two centimeters, which today is next to impossible to accomplish.

The minds of all that helped in the construction of Giza were directed by the wisdoms of Higher Consciousness. There is no other way such an architectural monument of energetic perfection could have been made. Over 2,300,000 stones were flawlessly used to complete Higher Consciousness' second sanctuary. Their aggregate weight is in excess of 15 billion pounds.

Today, many questions remain unanswered about Giza's construction. How could the workers make the pyramids faces so flat using only stone and copper tools?

How were the blocks made so uniform?

How was all this work completed in only 20 years?

How did the faces meet at such a perfect point at the summit?

How could the tiers be made so level?

How could some of the largest blocks be placed with such precession at such great heights?

How could millions of casing blocks all be made to fit perfectly?

How could so many workers maneuver on Giza's building site?

It's because Lucifer had turned off EGO and the workers of Giza were energetically directed by the wisdom of Higher Consciousness. Today, 4500 years later the minds of consciousness man have no idea how the making of Giza was completed with such pinpoint accuracy.

With Giza (Higher Consciousness' second sanctuary) complete Lucifer turned on his EGO chip again within the minds of Giza's workers. This placed their minds back in his energetic mind prison. The wisdom of Higher Consciousness that led its workers to build Giza during its 20-year construction was forever blotted out from their minds when EGO was turned back on by Lucifer.

Lucifer knew this impressive structure was Higher Consciousness' second sanctuary through which its Divine Child would begin its energy birth on December 21, 2082.

Lucifer knew he has until December 21, 2082 to ignite the missing capstone of Giza to complete Higher Consciousness' *No. 7* energy labor.

Lucifer knew he had to create a two-step energy process in order to accomplish this. His first step was to create the required energy force to ignite Giza. He believes he has successfully completed this through his drug of money. His plans can be seen on the reverse side of the American one-dollar bill. Energetically, Lucifer owns everything money has produced. He believes this energy is the force that will ignite Giza's missing capstone.

His intentions are in plain view for everyone to see. They are beneath his Seeing Eye capstone on the back of the American one-dollar bill marked out in plain view as the Latin phrase *Novus Ordo Seclorum*, which means "New Order of the Ages." Lucifer believes his drug of money is the new order of the ages force that will energetically ignite Giza's missing capstone so that Higher Consciousness' energy labor can be completed through his *illuminati* on December 21, 2082.

On January 1, 2000 Lucifer tried unsuccessfully to symbolically add Giza's missing capstone by having a helicopter lower a 30-foot high gold-encased capstone on top of Giza. It was Lucifer's attempt to confirm to his 144,000 *illuminati* family that he and they are Giza's missing capstone energy. For reasons that remain a mystery to consciousness man and only known by Higher Consciousness this was not allowed to happen.

Higher Consciousness placed its symbolic significance and purpose inside of Giza during its construction 4500 years ago. It was discovered in 1954 and is Higher Consciousness' solar barge.

Higher Consciousness' solar barge was discovered in 1954, undisturbed in a sealed pit of Giza. It is a vessel intended to carry the ascended through the Universe.

Higher Consciousness' solar barge symbolically represents its energy shuttle that will be energetically activated through the energetic igniting of Giza's capstone.

Higher Consciousness' solar barge is its energy shuttle that will be energetically activated by at least 144,000 incarnated beings.

When 144,000 have completed their deification process and been completely incarnated as Higher Consciousness Giza will be energetically turned to begin its energy shuttle's igniting.

Higher Consciousness' 144,000 (minimum) first sanctuaries that have attained their deifications will have a reserved seat on Higher Consciousness' energy shuttle.

Higher Consciousness' energy concert, third movement, minuet and trio, *Symphony No. 7* completes on December 21, 2082 at 11:11:10 GMT.

CHAPTER 46

THE RONDO SYMPHONIES

HIGHER CONSCIOUSNESS' ENERGY CONCERT fourth and final movement rondo begins on December 21, 2082 at 11:11:11 GMT with the unlocking of its *Symphony No. 8*. This is also Higher Consciousness' eighth master force.

Rondos are fast and vivacious. They will be no different for Higher Consciousness' energy concert rondo. Its ending rondo consists of its eighth, ninth and tenth energy symphonies that are its eighth, ninth and tenth master forces.

Giza is situated on Earth's divine energetic portal. It is Earth's most sacred site that when activated is the spot where Earth will first connect with the divine realm. It was where Jesus was protected from Lucifer for nearly 15 years before his ministry began. Jesus spent countless hours perched at the top of Giza's missing capstone communicating directly with Higher Consciousness preparing for his forthcoming ministry. Here he learned everything about Higher Consciousness's energy pregnancy and deification process for his forthcoming ministry.

Higher Consciousness' *Symphony No. 8* and eighth master force begins its Divine Child's energy birth. With the energy shuttle ignited by Higher Consciousness deified great multitude who attained their deification, it will energetically leave its pre-birth home of Giza and find its pre-destined location above Giza.

Here it will wait for the ascended. The ascended will than begin their physical ascension from every corner of the world and enter the waiting Higher Consciousness energy shuttle above Giza.

Inside the shuttle, all of the ascended will find their reserved seats. Inside will be Eden, the utopian paradise that Higher Consciousness had prepared for Adam and Eve 6000 years ago. There will be no restrictions or limitations.

During the 1000 year journey, the defied will individually be led to their personal pyramids around the Universe that Higher Consciousness had built in its energy fetus' 13.72 billion year gestation. The capstones of these pyramids will be unlit.

First, the ascended will begin by igniting the pyramids on Earth above and below the oceans. Next, the energy shuttle will venture to the Moon where all of its pyramids will be ignited. As each pyramid is lit, they will create a violet light that will shoot straight up from the ignited capstone and reach the edge of the Universe. For 1000 years, each ascended individual will become a sky-walker and individually leave the energy shuttle to ignite their prescribed pyramid within the Universe.

As each of the ascended leaves the energy shuttle to ignite their pyramid; the remaining ascended will watch with great joy and pride as their ascended brothers and sisters light their personal pyramid capstones throughout the Universe.

Higher Consciousness will lead its energy shuttle through every atom in the Universe during its 1000-year journey. As it does, every atom's missing symmetrical antimatter mirror image of divine energy energetic perfection and perfect love antimatter that had been removed by Higher Consciousness (because of Lucifer's betrayal) will be restored by Higher Consciousness. Behind the energy shuttle it will produce a violet trail of radiation because of the matter and antimatter's reunification. This energy will propel the energy shuttle on its 1000-year journey.

The violet lights of every ignited pyramid will be visible within the Universe from the energy shuttle. When all of the ascendants' pyramids are ignited, the Universe will be ready for its energy birth.

After 1000 years, the Universe will be energetically lit up as the full glory of Higher Consciousness' divine energy energetic perfection and perfect love. When complete Higher Consciousness energy shuttle will return to hover above Earth as its *Symphony No. 8* first rondo will end.

Higher Consciousness' first rondo will begin its energy birth not only in our Universe but also in all other 100 trillion energy cells of the energy fetus. The same 1000-year journey will simultaneously take place in every other Universe to prepare each and every energy cell for Higher Consciousness' energy birth.

On December 21, 3082 at 11:11:11 GMT Higher Consciousness' second rondo and *Symphony No. 9* will begin. In the energy shuttle Higher Consciousness' second fruits will arrive to be one with the ascended first fruits.

Then, in a flash, Higher Consciousness' energy shuttle will move to the edge of the Universe. There will be no movement felt inside the energy shuttle. Individually, each of the first ascended will grab their pyramid's violet light strings and hold them tight with their right hand. As each hold their pyramid's violet light strings, they will begin to pull with them the entire Universe. No divine energy atoms will be lost; every pyramid's ignited violet light are the energy strings that hold Higher Consciousness' energy balloon in place to secure every atoms future.

At this moment the energy shuttle and energy balloon of all of the Universe's violet energy atoms will go through the Sun and energy cervix of Higher Consciousness.

Upon reaching their landing spot on the other side, the first fruits will let go of their pyramid's violet light strings and release every violet energy atom from the Universe into its new home.

At this exact moment Higher Consciousness' second energy cell will also arrive on the other side. It too will unleash all of its violet energy atoms into its new home.

The two Universes will become one and double in size. Concurrently, all of the ascended will become one with their second energetic DNA strand.

When the souls and atoms of Higher Consciousness' first and second energy cells are complete; the Divine Child's first layer of energetic segmentation will have been completed. At this moment Higher Consciousness' Divine Child second layer of energetic segmentation will begin.

It will begin with the arrival of Higher Consciousness' third, fourth, fifth and sixth energy shuttles from Higher Consciousness' third, fourth, fifth and sixth energy fetus's energy cells that had just been birthed through its energy cervix.

When the third, fourth, fifth, sixth energy shuttles flawlessly touch down, its ascended will simultaneously let their pyramids ignited violet strings go.

Like Higher Consciousness' Divine Child first layer of energetic segmentation, each of the third, fourth, fifth and sixth energy shuttle's atoms will become one with Higher Consciousness' first layer of energetic segmentation.

At this moment Higher Consciousness' Divine Child will now be six times the size of what we know our Universe to be and our physical selves will have ignited our first six energetic DNA strands of Higher Consciousness divine energy.

Higher Consciousness' *Symphony No. 9* and second rondo movement will be complete after 45 similar layers of energetic segmentation.

As Higher Consciousness' Divine Child frolics about in its energetic paradise, no one will know when Higher Consciousness unlocks its tenth master force from its energy mind to close its energy womb forever.

Everyone will witness the Divine Child's heart being made. It begins with the triumphant entrance of Higher Consciousness who takes its rightful seat of power. Higher Consciousness' energy eyes of Jesus and Lucy next appear and take their deserved seats to the left and right of Higher Consciousness. The Divine Child's heart will now be prepared for all to commune, honor, respect and reign with forever and ever.

As Higher Consciousness' third eye you will have become the Divine Child's royal lifeblood as was Higher Consciousness energy pregnancies intent. As the Divine Child's royal lifeblood you are its host that ensures its survival. You will forevermore bring the Divine Child, its Higher Consciousness' energy nutrients to every one of its 100 trillion energy cells to aid in its infinite development from your royal lifeblood infinite heart communions.

PART VII:
THE SECRET
VARIABLE

CHAPTER 47

AUTHORIZING ORDER FROM CHAOS

"Whatever the mind can conceive and believe it
can achieve."
Napoleon Hill (1883–1970)

THE SACREDNESS OF HIGHER Consciousness is
so much more then theological restrictions and
limitations. It is so much more then science's
unanswered questions. It is the "at-one-ment" of the
two that completes both to unveil all that Higher
Consciousness is.

Higher Consciousness' energy pregnancy secret and
deification process has been unveiled so evil, pain and
suffering can be eliminated and its Divine Child can be
birthed.

We are in the midst of historical transformation that
will be led by the souls of mankind. They will move
us past our consciousness limitations to liberate us

and unleash our enhanced public ownership future and life. Everything begins with your deification that starts to eliminate today's prevailing energy of fear and negativity to extinguish evil.

Know that you are where you are supposed to be when your soul begins to awaken. Your age, sexual orientation, skin color, physical appearance or ethnic background matter not.

How much love you have for yourself and your flesh will be determined by your choice and authorization that allows Higher Consciousness to incarnate and become you. Higher Consciousness will never make you do anything other than what you feel is right. It will never violate any boundaries. Higher Consciousness' energy pregnancy blueprint has always intended your fate to be decided by you.

Consider this your official invitation to attend Higher Consciousness's infinite, immortal party of life.

Remember that as an angel energy thread of Higher Consciousness your soul is eternal and can never be destroyed. The worst it will be on the Divine Child is its angel self-minus your flesh. However, its purpose and evolution has always been to attain its archangel status by ascending your flesh.

When you make your decision always listen to that wee small voice from within, it will never lead you wrong.

Because of Lucifer's betrayal your authorization represents Higher Consciousness' only hope of eliminating evil and birthing its Divine Child.

Incarnation is everything Higher Consciousness can give to say thank you.

So what's it going to be? Yes or no?

Enjoy the journey!

www.ingramcontent.com/pod-product-compliance
Lightning Source LLC
Chambersburg PA
CBHW060240100426
42742CB00011B/1589